Comments about Sanford Mappa's book *How to Become Mortgage Free in Ten Years or Less, Without Extra Payments*

Sandy Mappa's excellent book shows us how to be mortgage free and achieve the American dream of owning your own home. Please read this book.
Dr. Dean Ornish, President and Director,
The Preventive Medicine Research Institute, and Author of
Dr. Dean Ornish's Program for Reversing Heart Disease
and *Eat More, Weigh Less*

Sandy Mappa's book provides clear insight into the often confusing world of mortgage management and financial planning. I thank him for it from my heart and wallet.
Dr. Lee Lipsenthal, Vice President and Medical Director,
The Preventive Medicine Research Institute

This is an excellent book for those people wanting to learn how to achieve the American dream of being mortgage free. Anyone with a mortgage who wants to become wealthy in today's economy *must* read this book!
Roy M. Strong, Radio Show Host,
Successful Financial Concepts

Fantastic book! If you apply Sandy Mappa's strategies, you'll be mortgage free sooner than you can ever imagine.
Ronald De Legge, President,
De Legge Real Estate Investments

This book contains very powerful information. Not only will you save a substantial amount of money and reduce your income taxes, but, by applying these easy-to-use strategies you will eliminate your biggest debt—your home mortgage—in less than ten years.
David S. Gilfand, Enrolled Agent and Accredited Tax Advisor

Fantastic! At last, a book that doesn't just tell you why but shows you how to eliminate your biggest nightmare—"debt payments."
Marshall Albarelli, Certified Financial Planner and Pension and Pre-Retirement Planning Advisor

Must reading for every homeowner.
David I. Ginsburg, President,
Loantech, a national mortgage consulting firm

Anyone who has a mortgage should read this book.
Paul Richard, Director of Education,
National Center for Financial Education

Sandy Mappa's principles and strategies will save you a fortune in money.
Scott E. Bretl, CPA

Sandy reveals the little-known facts that bankers have kept to themselves for decades. It's empowering.
Shawn P. Hickey, Principal, Wilmarc Financial Group

This book is outstanding, and easy to apply with no additional risks. You must read it!
Ronald J. Campbell, Radio Show Host,
Successful Business Hour

This book easily illustrates how thousands of dollars slip through our hands and how you can stop it. I call this required reading.
Ronald C. White, Attorney

Finally a book that shows us all how to save hundreds of thousands of dollars on our largest financial obligation—our mortgage.
John J. Gajkowski, Executive Vice President,
Money Managers Educational Services

I have been a CPA for 20 years. Sandy's book is based on sound financial and economic principles.
Alan P. Shaw, CPA

The mortgage and debt-free guru does it again. Sandy Mappa's book will educate you step by step. The "debt-weary" consumer should read this book over and over.
Edward Wilkens, Executive Vice President,
Capital Management Group, Inc.

Sandy has done mortgage holders and future mortgage holders a tremendous service! This is *the* textbook to teach the mortgage-free method!
Rolland Nielson, Licensed Mortgage Banker

To not read Sanford Mappa's book is a grave mistake—even if you don't have a mortgage.
Dr. Neil Garrett

You have provided the most powerful explanation I have encountered of the "lost future earnings cost."
Irwin F. Noparstak, CPA

This is a fantastic book that I *guarantee* will save everyone thousands of dollars and allow them to gain future financial security. This is a must read for everybody.

James W. Kerstein, Field Vice President,
Chubb LifeAmerica Insurance Company

This book is a must for any American who has a mortgage or is in the market to buy a house. You will save hundreds of thousands of dollars!

Dr. Mart McClellan and Dr. Lindsey McClellan

This book unlocks some of the misconceptions of true tax savings. The principles explained can save you thousands of dollars.

Charles S. Stoll, CPA, CFP

Wow! Sandy Mappa has produced a step-by-step guide toward the elimination of mortgage debt based on sound economic facts. Buy it! Read it!

John C. Stadler, Executive Vice President,
Capital Management Group, Inc.

The powerful information contained in this book will not only help home buyers and present homeowners choose the correct mortgage product, but will also let them learn the most important strategy of all: How to pay off their home earlier without making extra payments.

Edward Currie, Radio Show Host, *Home Buying Show*

HOW TO BECOME

MORTGAGE FREE

IN TEN YEARS OR LESS WITHOUT EXTRA PAYMENTS

- *42 Proven Strategies to Become Mortgage Free*
- *Substantially Reduce the Cost of Your Mortgage*
- *Save Thousands, Even* Hundreds of Thousands, *of Dollars*
- *10 Mortgage Misconceptions and 8 Mortgage Myths*
- *Reduce Your Income Taxes*
- *The Common Fallacy: Extra Payments Save You Money*
- *The Controversy: 15-Year Versus 30-Year Mortgages*
- *The Innovative Mortgage That Gives You Money Back*
- *The Best Time to Refinance*

BY SANFORD L. MAPPA

Library of Congress Catalog Card Number: 96-94388

ISBN: 0-9652058-0-0

Lunar Publishing
P.O. Box 2464
Glenview, IL 60025-6464

ACKNOWLEDGMENTS

It is impossible for me to personally mention everyone who has contributed to this book; however, I would especially like to thank:

David S. Gilfand, Enrolled Agent, Nationally Accredited Tax Advisor, (David S. Gilfand, Ltd., Deerfield, IL), for all of his priceless information;

Richard J. Freedkin, President, (R.J. Financial Services Mortgage Corporation, Arlington Heights, IL), for all of the important information he provided; and

Charles Stoll, Registered Investment Advisor, CPA, CFP, (Stoll Financial Corporation, Boca Raton, FL), for his invaluable advice.

Marcia L. Beinlich, deserves special mention. I sincerely appreciate all of her hard work, long hours, and devotion in helping me to complete this book.

Special thanks to my son, Mark A. Mappa, CFP, ChFC, CLU, RFC, CFS, (Glenview, IL), for his dedication, commitment, and assistance with this book.

Finally, no acknowledgment would be complete without grateful mention of my wife, Lynne, and daughter, Melissa. Their patience, kindness, loyalty, and love sustained me. Without them, this book would have been impossible to write.

CONTENTS

FOREWORD

One of the fastest-growing professions in the United States today is the field of financial planning. A home—and the mortgage that goes with it—is the biggest debt that most people will ever undertake. Financial planners provide help with investments, pensions, 401(k)s, individual retirement accounts (IRAs), stocks, bonds, real estate, taxes, annuities, saving for college, saving for retirement, life insurance, health insurance, and dozens of other financial issues that have a tremendous impact on the quality of a person's life and even his/her happiness. However, there is one extremely important area that financial planners have not paid sufficient attention to: helping Americans become mortgage free without making extra payments. *How to Become Mortgage Free in Ten Years or Less, Without Extra Payments* discusses the financial and psychological aspects of becoming mortgage free.

The financial issues that confront Americans today are so complex and the laws and regulations governing financial issues change so rapidly that many people feel overwhelmed. More and more people are turning to financial planners for advice and help in managing their finances and taxes.

I am proud to be a financial planner and I am happy that one of my sons has followed me into this honorable profession. During my career, I have worked hard to master many of the major fields of specialization in financial planning. I have earned eight professional designations and certifications: CFP (Certified Financial Planner), RFC (Registered Financial Consultant), AEP (Accredited Estate Planner), ChFC (Chartered Financial Consultant), CLU (Chartered Life Underwriter), RHU (Registered Health Underwriter), CFS (Certified Fund Specialist), and CIS (Certified Investment

Specialist). I am also a Registered Investment Advisor. This is not stated to impress you, but to impress upon you that I have done my homework and that I do thoroughly understand the field of financial planning. I have also developed a deep understanding of the psychological aspects of people's finances and of the importance of minimizing or eliminating personal debt.

I am not the only financial planner in the United States using the proven strategies discussed in this book. Recently, I began conducting nationwide educational seminars to teach my proven strategies to financial planners, insurance specialists, stock brokers, and mortgage brokers. If you would like to know the name of a financial planner in your area who can help you become mortgage free, call the American Institute for Money Management, Inc. (AIMM) at 800-729-AIMM, or write to AIMM, 1701 East Lake Avenue, Suite 400, Glenview, IL 60025.

I am 100% certain that my proven strategies for becoming mortgage free will work for you! They have worked for thousands of people, including myself. They are now working for other financial planners and their clients around the country. Best of all, you do not have to use all of these strategies to become mortgage free in ten years or less. Just using one or two of my strategies could put you in the position to be mortgage free in ten years or less. If you use three or four of my strategies simultaneously, you could actually be mortgage free in five to six years! Some of my clients are now in the position to become mortgage free after only four years. I am positive that after reading this book you will also be able to pay off your mortgage in ten years or less!

Sanford L. Mappa
President, American Institute for Money Management, Inc.
Glenview, Illinois

INTRODUCTION

How to Become Mortgage Free in Ten Years or Less, Without Extra Payments is a complete guide to Sandy Mappa's 42 proven strategies to become mortgage free. It is also designed to help you learn

- how to your maximize your tax deductions;
- why mortgage prepayments will not save you any money;
- how to choose the best type of mortgage for your financial situation;
- the lost future earnings* cost principle and how it applies to your home;
- how to reduce your income taxes;
- how to maximize the returns on your investments;
- how to make inflation work for you instead of against you; and
- much, much more.

How to Become Mortgage Free in Ten Years or Less, Without Extra Payments consists of the following 12 chapters:

- **Chapter 1: The History of Mortgages.** This chapter explains the history of mortgages since the time of the ancient Egyptians.
- **Chapter 2: Coming to Terms with Mortgages.** This chapter discusses the most essential mortgage terms.
- **Chapter 3: Eight Myths About Becoming Mortgage Free.** Each of these eight myths are analyzed.
- **Chapter 4: Ten Mortgage Misconceptions.** Here you will find out about ten misunderstandings related to mortgages and how to avoid those misunderstandings.

---

* *Lost future earnings* and *loss of future earnings* are interchangeable. In this book, we will use lost future earnings.

- **Chapter 5: The Best Time to Refinance Your Mortgage.** This chapter examines when it makes sense to refinance, how refinancing can help pay off your mortgage early, and the tax implications involved.
- **Chapter 6: How to Use Home Equity Loans to Your Advantage.** This chapter discusses when to take out a home equity loan and what you need to understand about them to obtain their maximum benefits.
- **Chapter 7: How to Make Inflation Your Ally Instead of Your Enemy.** Here I will help you use inflation to your advantage by choosing the right type of mortgage.
- **Chapter 8: The Mortgage Controversy: 15-Year Versus 30-Year Mortgages.** This chapter compares the advantages and disadvantages of a 15-year conventional mortgage to a 30-year conventional mortgage through examples.
- **Chapter 9: The Lost Future Earnings Cost.** You will be introduced to the critical money principle called the lost future earnings cost. The general public is unaware of this important money principle. Learn why your home costs substantially more than you realized. In addition, there are 28 tables that demonstrate the real cost of your home.
- **Chapter 10: The Investment Mortgage.** This is an innovative mortgage that gives you back money. The chapter also compares this type of mortgage with a conventional mortgage.
- **Chapter 11: Secrets of Mortgage Prepayment Strategies and Biweekly Mortgages.** I will explain four mortgage prepayment strategies including the biweekly mortgage, and the benefits and limitations of each. You will learn why these strategies will not save you any money.

- **Chapter 12: Forty-Two Strategies to Become Mortgage Free.** This chapter contains my proven strategies that will show you how to become mortgage free in ten years or less without extra payments.

How to Become Mortgage Free in Ten Years or Less, Without Extra Payments provides consumers, investors, financial planners, insurance professionals, accountants, lawyers, mortgage brokers and lending institutions with a complete understanding of the concepts and principles of using a mortgage to its fullest advantage.

CHAPTER 1

The History of Mortgages

> The borrower is the servant to the lender.
>
> –*Proverbs 22:7*
>
> There can be no freedom or beauty about a home life that depends on borrowing and debt.
>
> –Henrik Ibsen, *A Doll's House*

Have you ever asked yourself, "What is my largest financial commitment?" The answer should not surprise you. A mortgage is the largest financial commitment you may ever make in your life. When you stop to factor in the mortgage principal and the interest paid, as well as the lost future earnings* cost, many of you will spend more than $500,000 to pay off your $100,000 mortgage!

It is important to understand what it is that you are buying before you actually buy it. For example, you may spend hours learning about computers before deciding which system to buy. Patiently, you learn every detail about RAM and ROM, CD drives, streaming tape backup, flop-optical disks, and parallel and serial ports. All this effort for what amounts

---

* *Lost future earnings* and *loss of future earnings* are interchangeable. In this book, we will use lost future earnings. Chapter 9 will cover this money principle.

to a $2,000 purchase. Yet, you will go out and within 30 minutes make a quick decision on a $100,000 mortgage—a mortgage that could cost you $300,000 or more in principal and interest during the length of the mortgage. Most people spend months or years searching for their dream house and then spend almost no time at all in selecting their mortgage. This is a critical mistake which I will help you avoid.

I encourage you to take some time in learning the intricacies of mortgages. Spending a few hours of your time learning about mortgages will be time well spent. Along the way you will begin to understand how a mortgage should form the centerpiece of your financial plan. Learning the concept and structure of mortgages will enable you to make the right decision. You need not mortgage your financial future if you learn to turn your mortgage into an investment in your future.

The History

The word mortgage comes from the French words *mort* meaning "dead" and *gage* meaning "pledge." The history of mortgages is, to a large degree, the recorded history of mankind. To own land and property is one of the strongest of all human desires. More wars have been fought over land ownership than anything else in human history.

The desire to own land and to regulate its transfer is so strong that it has been an influential force behind the development of laws, contracts, and even the United States government. People have always instinctively understood that the person who owns land controls power. In all ancient societies, those who owned land controlled food and supplies because they controlled the farms. Land is the original storehouse of all wealth. Remember that even gold, silver, and diamonds come from the land—as does almost all of our food. Is it any wonder why people want to own land?

Egypt. While it was originally valued for its ability to produce food and as the basis for the building of homes and communities, land soon became viewed as a primary form of wealth and security. Land was used as security as far back as the settlement of Babylonia and Egypt. These ancient civilizations actually developed many of the basic principles still used today in mortgage lending: naming the borrower, naming the lender, and legally describing the property. The ancient Egyptians were the first to survey land because the annual flooding of the Nile River wiped out property markers.

Greece. The ancient Greeks further developed the concept of mortgage lending. It was in Greece that temple leaders often loaned money with real estate being held as security. This shows that, very early on and in many succeeding societies, religious groups took a strong interest in real estate activities.

Roman Empire. The Roman Empire elevated real estate lending to the level of an art form. The Romans developed the concept of *fiducia,* which refers to the transfer of possession and land title. Fiducia dictated that if a borrower fulfilled his/her obligation, a reconveyance or transferring back would occur. A variation of this concept developed later as a new concept of security came into acceptance: It was called *pigmus.* Instead of transferring a title, the land was pawned. Although the title and possession remained with the borrower, the lender had the right to take possession of the property at any time it was determined that the possibility of default existed.

The ancient Romans also developed the concept that would later evolve into what we now call *foreclosure.* This concept stated that if the borrower failed to pay on his/her mortgage, permanent conveyance of the title would occur. In other words, if the borrower did not pay his/her mortgage debt as required, the borrower could lose title to the property. As common as this concept is today, at one time it did not exist. The development of this concept, which was originally called *hypotheca,* changed the course of human history.

Dark Ages. During the Dark Ages, the Germans developed a new concept in mortgage law: It was called gage. This concept basically stated that if the borrower defaulted on his/her mortgage, the lender had to look exclusively to the property for fulfillment of the debt. In other words, the lender could not go after the individual, only after the property. This was a very positive development in the history of lending. This concept still applies in many states today. Be sure to check with your attorney to verify if it applies in your state.

After the Dark Ages, the feudal system took hold. In this system of government, the king had absolute control and was the owner of nearly all the land. The king granted the use of land to his lords in return for their military support. If a lord ceased to perform this military service, or if he died, the king took back the use of the land. Once again, land was used as security for the performance of an obligation. In this case, the obligation was not monetary repayment of a debt, but rather repayment of a military obligation.

England. In England, the Catholic Church was very powerful and influential. The Catholic Church took the position that charging any amount of interest on a loan was unethical. For that reason, there were few mortgage loans in England. Would you loan money if you could not charge interest? Most of the loans that were given were not to buy land or houses, but were for the purpose of a farmer's purchase of pigs, cattle, or seed for the fields. Since interest could not be charged, the farmer would pledge part of the fields as security. The lender actually took possession and title of the pledged fields and received all rents and profits. If the borrower did not repay the debt as specified, the lender would get permanent title to that portion of the fields the farmer had pledged. After being fully repaid, the lender reconveyed the title to the borrower.

Under the English system, borrowers had almost an unlimited amount of time to redeem their property. In other words, whenever they paid off the money that was owed, the borrower could get the property back. This made it difficult for the lender to do any long-term planning or development of the property. In 16th century England, laws were enacted that gave the borrower a limited amount of time, usually six months, to pay his/her debts and redeem his/her property, or lose all rights to it.

United States. The United States has contributed several unique developments to the world of mortgage lending, including land development banks, thrift institutions, the loan correspondent system, and annual percentage rates, just to name a few. With the westward expansion of the United States, property purchases were financed by land development banks. Unfortunately, there was much speculation in land and nearly all of the land development banks quickly went bankrupt.

In the early 1800s, many Americans continued to live on small farms. What little mortgage lending that had occurred was primarily done through arrangements between friends and among family members.

In 1816 the first thrift institution was formed in the United States: the Philadelphia Savings Fund Society. In 1831 another significant step in mortgage lending occurred: The Oxford Provident Building Association was organized in Pennsylvania. The Oxford Provident Building Association allowed its organizers the opportunity of obtaining funds with which to purchase homes. As other similar associations were formed, they became a popular means of financing home purchases throughout the United States.

However, thrift institutions took a long time getting established as major lenders, partly because they simply did not have much money to lend.

As the nation continued to expand westward and settle the middle west region, there was a tremendous need for money with which to purchase this new land. Simultaneously, on the East Coast, large insurance companies and wealthy individuals were looking for ways to invest their money, and needed a way to originate loans. These two needs evolved into today's mortgage loan correspondent system. Many of the biggest mortgage loan companies developed in the Midwest.

It was not until 1913 that the Federal Reserve Act authorized federally chartered banks to be able to lend money on real estate. Still, most of the loans granted were for farm property or for small business property. There were relatively few mortgages being granted for single-family homes. However, all this was about to change. In 1923 the Farm Mortgage Bankers Association changed its name to the Mortgage Bankers Association. Not only did it change its name, it changed its emphasis to residential lending.

Home mortgage lending was, in some ways, still primitive. The maximum loan-to-equity value was 50%, meaning that you could only borrow $5,000 should your house cost $10,000. In addition, the loan had to be repaid in three to five years. There was no provision to amortize the loan. Interest payments were made twice a year. Most loans were refinanced every three to five years because people did not have the money to pay them off. Lenders charged between 1% and 3% of the loan as a fee, and every time the loan was refinanced, they charged an additional 1%.

The Roaring Twenties was a period of great optimism in the United States. For the first five years, real estate prices appreciated 25% to 50% a year in many areas of the country.

For example, a $10,000 home might have been worth $15,000 a year later. Lenders abandoned their underwriting guidelines, thinking that rising prices would be able to save any loan.

The real estate market began to decline in 1927 and property values fell dramatically. As with any form of speculation, there was risk involved and many fortunes were lost. Those investors who did not lose money in real estate began to heavily invest their money in the stock market, which seemed to offer maximum profit for minimal work. In 1929, the illusory values of the stock market were exposed and America experienced a huge, painful stock market crash in which many Americans lost almost all of their net worth. This stock market crash then led to a massive psychological and economic depression in the United States, with the official rate of unemployment reaching 25%.

During the Great Depression, banks and thrift institutions had very little money to lend out. Foreclosures became common. The highest number of foreclosures occurred from 1931 to 1935, averaging 250,000 each year. By 1935, through foreclosures, banks and thrift institutions owned 20% of all the real estate on which they had made loans. In fact, many of these foreclosures were actually caused by second- and third-position mortgage holders who had panicked. Borrowers, increasingly angry about this epidemic of foreclosures, reacted with hysteria and mild violence. This caused some of the lenders to voluntarily begin the practice of forbearance (a delay in enforcing foreclosures), which caused laws to be created. Iowa became the first state to enact a law that suspended almost all foreclosures. During the next year and a half, 27 states enacted laws that curtailed or suspended the use of foreclosure. In the early 1940s, as real estate prices once again began their ascent, all of these moratorium laws were expunged.

In 1934, the Federal Housing Administration (FHA) was created, which introduced mortgage insurance and self-amortizing mortgages. In 1944, the Veterans Administration (VA) began granting VA loans to veterans that were guaranteed by the government. In 1965, the Department of Housing and Urban Development (HUD) was created to oversee all real estate and mortgage lending. In 1968, the Consumer Credit Protection Act required banks and thrift institutions to fully disclose the actual annual percentage rate (APR) on loans. This made it possible, for the first time, to objectively compare one loan to another, providing a major advantage for borrowers.

In 1974, the Equal Credit Opportunity Act was created to prohibit discrimination in lending based on sex, marital status, age, race, color, national origin, or religion.

Similar to the period of the 1920s, an unfavorable real estate market in the 1980s was followed by a stock market crash. In 1981, lenders had the highest interest rates in the history of the United States: The prime rate hit an astonishing 21½%! When the prime rate reached its all-time high, stock brokerage firms and mutual fund companies began a campaign of heavy advertising and aggressive marketing. This increased awareness on the part of investors caused record amounts of stock market and investment transactions. In 1987, the greatest stock market crash in history occurred with a loss of more than 500 points in one day.

No one has a crystal ball and no one can predict what will happen next to the economy. However, by studying history, we can learn and be aware of the warning signs of over-speculation. There is a saying that unsuccessful people learn from their mistakes, whereas highly successful people learn from the mistakes of others. I want you to be highly successful, especially in paying off the biggest debt you may ever have: your home mortgage!

This brief history should have provided you with a deeper understanding of where mortgages came from, the cyclical nature of real estate, and the ever changing rules and laws of mortgage lending.

An Extremely Important Reason To Be in the Position To Become Mortgage Free

You are probably astonished at the number of changes that have taken place in mortgage lending in just the past 100 years. In this century, mortgage rates have fluctuated greatly, ranging from 5% to more than 20% per year. At times, real estate prices have escalated and they have also collapsed, but in general, the value of real estate has increased each decade.

During the Civil War, both the Union and the Confederacy imposed income taxes. The Federal income tax system that now exists was enacted in 1913, shortly after the passage of the 16th Amendment, which allowed for the imposition of an income tax. In 1913, there was a flat tax. Married couples were taxed at a rate of 1% on income over $4,000 and single taxpayers on income over $3,000. High income earners paid a surtax of 6%. The median yearly income in 1913 was $620. Only 2% of the people in the United States paid any federal income tax. The majority of the United States government's revenue came from excise taxes and customs duties, which accounted for 90% of the revenue. In the early 1920s, the tax code began to undergo frequent legislative changes.

What will be the next major change? Today, your home mortgage interest deduction is already being threatened. Some congressmen actually want to eliminate the home mortgage interest deduction entirely. Currently, based on your tax bracket and other tax considerations, you may be able to deduct interest on mortgages up to $1,000,000*—see your tax advisor for your personal situation. It was not too long ago that you could deduct an unlimited amount of interest.

What would happen to your finances if you could not deduct your home mortgage interest payments? This change could cause your net spendable income to be reduced.

The congressmen who are arguing for the elimination of this interest deduction are very powerful and persuasive. They argue that many other countries have no home mortgage interest deduction. Most importantly, they say that the elimination of this deduction, which in the aggregate amounts to billions of dollars of lost tax revenue, is one way the government can help balance the budget.

Be prepared. If the home mortgage interest deduction is reduced or even eliminated, people who cannot substantially pay down or pay off their mortgage will feel the financial strain. But, if you follow the proven principles revealed in this book, you will soon be in the position to pay down or pay off your home mortgage. Then any changes the government makes will have a minimal affect on you.

---

*In addition to the interest on a mortgage up to $1,000,000, you can also deduct interest up to $100,000 through an equity loan. For more information, see Chapters 5 and 6.

CHAPTER 2

Coming to Terms With Mortgages

Debt is a grievous bondage to an honorable man.
–Publilius Syrus

Be not make a beggar by banqueting upon borrowing.
–Ecclesiasticus, xviii, 33

In my 20-year career as a certified financial planner, I have discovered that many people who take out home mortgages do not understand basic mortgage terms. For example, with little knowledge of the terms to which they are about to agree, people rush out and acquire a mortgage. Then, years later, they stop to wonder why their monthly payments are so high and why they have made so little progress in paying down that mortgage. The sad part is, had these people taken the time to learn mortgage basics, there would be no mystery to the process and they would have found the mortgage that worked to their financial advantage.

Therefore, the more you know about them, the more mortgages can work for you and not against you. The more you know about the types of mortgages and understand mortgage terms, the more you can convert this knowledge to your financial benefit in finding a mortgage that is exactly right for you.

From reading about the history of mortgages in Chapter 1, you now know that mortgage means "dead" (mort) "pledge" (gage). A lender called a *mortgagee* lends money to the borrower called a *mortgagor* who pledges land or improvements (such as a house or building) as security for repayment of the debt. The borrower then pays interest. If the borrower defaults and does not perform as specified in the mortgage contract, the lender can foreclose and take possession and ownership of the property, or sell it for the unpaid debt. When the debtor pays off the creditor, the mortgage and the debt are eliminated. Let us now review the most essential mortgage terms.

Conventional Mortgage

Traditionally, a conventional mortgage is made by a private institution or lender and is not insured nor guaranteed by the government. Today, many conventional mortgages are purchased by government chartered corporations, which are part of the secondary mortgage market. The secondary mortgage market buys and sells existing mortgages to fund the housing market. It includes three quasi-government agencies: (1) the Federal National Mortgage Association, which is known as Fannie Mae; (2) the Federal Home Loan Mortgage Corporation, which is known as Freddie Mac; and (3) the Government National Mortgage Association, which is known as Ginnie Mae.

There are two additional government agencies you will learn more about later in this chapter: the Federal Housing Administration (FHA) and the Veterans Administration (VA), both of which help home buyers on the primary mortgage market by insuring or guaranteeing residential mortgage loans.

Nowadays, the term "conventional loan" has come to describe all those mortgages other than the FHA or VA government-insured loans.

30-Year and 15-Year Mortgages

A 30-year mortgage is paid off or amortized over 30 years and a 15-year mortgage is paid off or amortized over 15 years. The difference between the two is that if a home buyer takes out a 15-year mortgage, the monthly payments will be higher, the house will be paid off quicker, and the interest rate will probably be slightly lower than with a 30-year mortgage. Chapter 8 discusses in detail the comparison of the 15-year and 30-year mortgage. The results may surprise you!

Interest

We all have an interest in interest. Interest is payment for the use of money. This concept has been around for centuries. When we are considering a mortgage or, for that matter, any other loan or debt, we usually think of ourselves as victims of circumstance because of the interest we pay to our creditors. However, many advantages accrue to the person who pays interest. First of all, mortgage interest is tax deductible. The IRS defines home mortgage interest as "any interest you pay on a loan secured by your home (main home or second home)." These loans include a mortgage to buy your home, a second mortgage, a line of credit or a home equity loan. In fact, the mortgage interest deduction is one of the only safe tax deductions remaining. Consider the fact that if you are in the 25% federal tax bracket, the government is effectively paying one-quarter of the cost of interest on the money borrowed. Therefore, the real rate of interest paid is only 75% of what the lender charges. If you borrow $100,000 at 8% interest, then you will be paying $8,000 in interest charges in the first year. Therefore, your actual out-of-pocket interest expense is only $6,000 (25% x $8,000). I advise you to check with your tax advisor to find out if mortgage interest is deductible in your state. If it is, this will even further reduce your cost of interest and will also increase your tax deductions.

The borrower will also benefit by the appreciated value of his/her newly acquired asset. Let us say that you buy a home for $120,000, and your down payment is $20,000. If real estate prices rose 10% in your first year of ownership, the value of your home would appreciate to $132,000—a gain of $12,000. Congratulations, you have already made 60% on your money ($12,000 gain ÷ $20,000 down payment). Now, if real estate prices only go up 5% in your first year of ownership, you have still made 30% on your money. I ask you, how many years do you have to leave your money in a savings account or certificate of deposit to earn 30%? How many years do you have to wait for your stocks to go up 30% or 60%? Because of the leverage that real estate offers, even a small gain in real estate prices leads to a tremendous compound rate of return on your down payment. Best of all, you do not pay any current taxes on the appreciated value.

As you can see, borrowing money and paying interest can be to your advantage, if you do it intelligently. Here is another example. If you rented a $120,000 home in many parts of the country, you would have to pay approximately $1,000 a month in rent, or $12,000 a year. If you buy a home, and the mortgage payments are $1,000 a month, ($12,000 a year, $8,000 in interest charges) your net interest cost, after the tax deduction, is only $6,000 if you are in the 25% tax bracket. Can you now see how you come out way ahead by paying interest?

Therefore, do not think of yourself as a victim because you have to pay the lender tax-deductible interest to borrow money. Remember also, due to inflation, you are paying the lender back with cheaper and cheaper dollars. If inflation is 4% a year, the money you pay back this year is worth 4% less than the dollars you paid back last year. The money you pay the lender in two years will be worth 8% less than the dollars you paid them this year. This further lowers your cost of borrowing. Taking out a mortgage to buy valuable real estate can make you a victor not a victim.

Remember that interest rates are set in the marketplace by the laws of supply and demand. The interest rate a lender charges a borrower is based on many factors, some of which include the lender's cost of funds, how much money the lender has available, how much competition the lender has, and how much risk the lender is assuming. Interest rates change frequently. By intelligent shopping, you will be able to get the best interest rate that is available at the time.

Points

Mortgage lenders often charge borrowers points in addition to mortgage application fees. One point equals 1% of the amount of the mortgage. On a $100,000 mortgage, two points will cost you $2,000. The points on a mortgage will be an additional deduction above the mortgage interest deduction. Deducting the points can be spread out over the term of the mortgage. If you refinance, however, the points paid must be deducted over the duration of the new mortgage.

Some lenders have no point mortgages. Are they a good buy? It depends. Remember, there is no free lunch. If you pay low points or no points, the lender makes up for it somewhere else. In almost every case, the lender will charge you a higher interest rate if you get a low point or no point mortgage.

If you plan to stay in the house for at least five years, it may be to your advantage to pay higher initial costs (more points) in exchange for lower long-term costs (lower interest rates). On the other hand, if you plan to move within two or three years, you would want to minimize your initial costs. Also, your decision may be affected by how much money you have available to pay points versus your ability to make payments over the term of the mortgage. The annual percentage rate will give you a more accurate picture of what your actual year-after-year cost of the mortgage is.

Annual Percentage Rate (APR)

The APR will show you the total cost of a mortgage, including points, interest, and closing costs. This cost is stated as an interest rate. The purpose of the APR is to compare the costs of different types of mortgages. An adjustable-rate mortgage is very difficult to compare because the interest rate will change during the length of the mortgage. Furthermore, your tax bracket will have an affect on the net cost of the APR.

Many lenders advertise a very low interest rate to get your attention. For example, you might read your local newspaper today and see an ad for a mortgage with an interest rate of only 4%. However, this may be the introductory rate, which is only good for the first six months. Sometimes this introductory rate is called the "sucker rate." In addition, this introductory rate does not include the points, fees, or origination costs of the mortgage. When all of those fees are factored into the APR, you can arrive at the true cost of the mortgage. Always look at the APRs when comparing mortgages. Do not pay much attention to the introductory rates.

Amortization

Amortization is repaying a debt in regular installments until the debt expires. A home mortgage allows you to amortize or pay back the principal you borrowed from a lender through regular monthly payments. Part of each payment will be interest and the balance will be used to pay back the principal. The mortgage balance decreases by the amount of principal applied from each payment.

Negative Amortization. This occurs when monthly mortgage payments are not large enough to pay all of the interest due. With negative amortization, you do not pay down your mortgage principal, but you actually add to it. You can end up owing more than the amount you originally borrowed. This can occur because your monthly mortgage payment does not sufficiently cover the current interest charges. You have the choice of increasing your monthly payment or extending the term of your mortgage, for example from 30 to 33 years. Avoid negative amortization whenever possible. Negative amortization does not occur with conventional fixed-rate mortgages.

Down Payment

The down payment is the upfront cash you will pay toward the purchase of your home. The down payment reduces the amount of the purchase price that will need to be financed. Upon purchase, the down payment signifies the buyer's equity in the property. Generally, the larger the down payment, the lower the monthly payments. The standard down payment is 20%. With a down payment of less than 20%, private mortgage insurance will usually be added to the mortgage. This will increase your monthly payments. Home buyers can put down as little as 3% on conventional and Federal Housing Administration mortgages. Even lower amounts are allowed by the Veterans Administration.

Private Mortgage Insurance (PMI)

This form of insurance protects the lender, not the borrower, against the possibility of a mortgage default. PMI might be required if you have a poor credit history, if you went bankrupt, or if you are buying a home and making a small down payment. Almost all lenders require PMI unless you make at least a 20% down payment. You have to pay for this PMI which is added to your monthly mortgage payment.

Fixed-Rate Mortgage (FRM)

FRMs are mortgages made at a predetermined fixed-rate of interest that never changes over the duration of the mortgage.

FRMs include 30-year and 15-year mortgages, as well as graduated payment and growing equity mortgages.

FRMs do have some advantages. Most individuals' income will rise over the years. Because 30-year and 15-year monthly mortgage payments remain constant, when a person's income does increase he/she will have more disposable income. FRMs do have an advantage in a rising interest rate environment. When interest rates are going up, homeowners with ARMs will pay increased interest rates, and people with FRMs will not.

Fixed-rate mortgages also have some disadvantages. As interest rates decrease, people who have fixed-rate mortgages have to pay whatever high interest rates they started with. Some people who obtained mortgages in the early 1980s were paying 16% and 17% interest rates. Refinancing to a lower, fixed-interest rate, or an adjustable rate mortgage (ARM) should be considered under these circumstances.

Adjustable-Rate Mortgage (ARM)

Adjustable-rate mortgages became popular in the 1980s. Unlike a fixed-rate mortgage that has a constant, predictable fixed-rate and monthly payment, an ARM's interest rate—and payment—increases or decreases during the length of the mortgage. Changes in the interest rate are tied to an established index, which the lender does not control. Lenders base their interest rates on a particular index plus a margin. Your lender will choose a certain index to serve as a guide in calculating the periodic interest rate adjustment. If the index increases, so does the interest rate on your mortgage and also your monthly payments will be higher. What will happen if the index rate decreases? Your mortgage interest rate will be decreased as well as your monthly mortgage payment. To help determine the cost of the principal and interest portion of your monthly mortgage payments, ask your lender to compute three hypothetical situations: 1) the worst case—when the interest rate rises to the highest possible level, 2) the best case—a low and stable interest rate, and 3) the past performance—based on the historical fluctuations of the interest rate.

The major advantage offered by ARMs is that they usually have lower initial interest rates than fixed-rate mortgages. For example, if fixed-rates are 9%, you may be able to get an ARM with an initial interest rate of 7%. Borrowers who took out ARMs saw their mortgage rates and payments drop sometimes quite substantially. Thus, these people had more disposable, spendable income each month. In the early 1990s, it was actually possible to get ARMs that started at only a little over 5% interest. When you consider the fact that this interest is tax deductible, the actual cost for borrowing mortgage money was extremely low.

The disadvantage of ARMs is that interest rates can increase. The ARM that you started out with at 7% may go up to 10% should interest rates rise. Had you taken out a fixed-rate 9% mortgage, you would still be paying only 9%. While you will benefit from the lower initial rate that can be obtained with an ARM, you assume the risk of rising rates and rising monthly mortgage payments.

Index

An ARM's interest rate can increase or decrease according to a nationally recognized index. Some indexes are more volatile than others. The particular index that is used can make a considerable difference between adjustment periods. The lender has several choices of indexes they can use. They will explain which indexes they offer and what each index is based on. You should understand how the index being used will affect your mortgage. Ask for a past history of how the index has performed. Lenders prefer to use a short to medium-term index (rates that change weekly or monthly) because it can measure the expectation of inflation. Lenders must use an index that they have no control over; for example, they cannot use their own prime rate. A few common indexes are

- the rates on one-year, three-year, and five-year U.S. Treasury securities and
- the Federal Home Loan Bank Board's national or regional average mortgage rate.

Some indexes, such as the one-year Treasury securities, are easy to follow.

Margin

A margin is the number of percentage points the lender adds to the index to determine what rate to charge you. One way of looking at the margin is to see it as the lender's profit or markup. Usually the lender will add one to three points. The index may be 4½% and the lender may add a margin of 2½% and charge you 7% interest on your mortgage. While the index may increase or decrease, the margin will never change over the length of the mortgage. When you compare ARMs, review both the index and the margin.

Adjustment Period

The time period between interest rate changes is called the adjustment interval or adjustment period. Depending on how an ARM was created, the adjustment period can range from six months, one year, three years, and five years. The most common are six months and one year. Longer adjustment periods are more stable, which makes it easier for borrowers to plan their finances. In return they usually have a higher interest rate.

Introductory Rate

The terms *introductory rate*, *initial rate*, *starting rate*, *teaser rate*, or *discounted rate* are often used interchangeably to describe an ARM's initial interest rate, which is usually several points below the fully indexed rate. The initial rate may be good for one month or up to one year. Most commonly, the introductory rate lasts six months or one year. After that, you will begin paying the fully indexed rate. For example, you may be able to find introductory rates as low as 4½% on ARMs. After six months, you will be paying a fully indexed rate of 7%. Be cautious of an initial interest rate that is much lower than the competition. These rates may be attractive now but could cost you a lot more in the very near future. For example, they may not have any rate limits for the first adjustment period. If an adjustment increase is made, your mortgage payments will increase. Low introductory rates can cause negative amortization.

Caps

Interest rate caps protect the borrower by limiting the amount that interest rates and monthly payments can increase. A payment cap will limit the amount of your mortgage payment by how much it can increase or decrease, usually in terms of a percentage of a previous monthly payment. A lender may also decide to protect its own interest by establishing a floor rate, which is a minimum interest rate. If the index rate plus the margin is less than the floor interest rate, the borrower will pay the floor interest rate. A periodic interest rate cap limits the amount that the interest rate and monthly payment can vary from one adjustment period to another. For example, many ARMs have 2% annual caps. This means that your mortgage cannot increase or decrease by more than 2% in a given year. If your mortgage is at 7%, it will be no more than 9% and no less than 5% at the end of the year. The lifetime cap is the maximum interest rate you can be charged at any time during the length of the mortgage. If you have a 7% mortgage with a 12% lifetime cap, you will never have to pay more than 12% interest.

When there is an increase in the interest rate that is limited by a cap, there will be a "catch-up" rate or payment that will probably occur in the following adjustment period, even if the indexed rates have not increased. As you can see, it is important to learn how caps can affect your mortgage.

Balloon Mortgage

A balloon mortgage is only available with a fixed-rate. The distinguishing feature of the balloon mortgage is that the entire principal of this short-term mortgage must be paid after three to seven years, depending on the arrangements you have made with your lender. The payments are based on a 30-year mortgage. Since most people cannot pay the full balance at the end of the balloon mortgage, they usually end up refinancing or getting a new mortgage. Some lenders will offer automatic refinancing as one of the terms of the mortgage contract. However, you will have to pay new refinancing charges. Balloon mortgages are not fully amortized—if they were, there would be no balloon payment due at the end.

An advantage of balloon mortgages is that they frequently have a slightly lower interest rate and lower payments. The lender incurs relatively little interest rate risk because of the short time period. This type of mortgage can make sense if you do not expect to live in your home for a long time, for example, if you plan to sell your house in a few years or your employer is going to relocate you. It may also be of interest to you if you have other uses for your money or if you will be receiving a lump sum of cash at the end of the balloon period.

Government-Assisted Mortgages

There are four main government-assisted mortgages: the Federal Housing Administration (FHA), the Veterans Administration (VA), the Farmer's Home Administration (FmHA) and state mortgage agencies. These are the major sources of government-assisted mortgages for home buyers. Check with your local lender about the different limits and qualifications in your area. Some states have housing finance agencies that will make available below-market interest rate mortgages for first-time home buyers. These mortgages have certain qualifications and limitations.

Federal Housing Administration (FHA). The FHA encourages home ownership for low and moderate income consumers by insuring mortgages. The FHA insures the mortgage that a lender will make by issuing an insurance policy. These mortgages must meet specific requirements, such as loan amounts and property standards. Down payments as low as 3% are required on FHA mortgages. Limits and requirements do change, so check with your lender for current qualifications.

The FHA offers 15-year and 30-year mortgages. These mortgages may be assumable and might have lower interest rates than conventional mortgages. FHA mortgages are easier to qualify for than conventional mortgages. If you incur some temporary financial difficulty and cannot make the monthly mortgage payments, you can apply to your lender for forbearance. Your mortgage may be extended for up to ten years to help lower your payments depending on your particular circumstances.

The FHA requires the borrower to pay part of the costs of the insurance. The buyer cannot finance points as part of the mortgage, so he/she must have the money available. If the buyer does not have the cash, the seller can pay the points. The amounts offered on FHA mortgages are less than what you can borrow on conventional mortgages.

Veterans Administration (VA). The VA guarantees that mortgages or a portion of them will be paid. The VA will only guarantee payment if the property meets its requirements and standards. The borrower (veteran) may use the mortgage for several reasons, such as to buy, build or pay for remodeling, improvements or repairs. The VA guarantee covers only a set amount, which changes over time. Veterans Administration mortgages require no down payment for certain amounts borrowed. When these borrowed amounts are exceeded, then there is a minimum down payment required. They are easier to qualify for and the interest rates may be lower than conventional mortgages. The amount of money you can borrow on a VA mortgage will be less than you can obtain from a conventional mortgage. The VA offers 15-year and 30-year mortgages.

Farmer's Home Administration (FmHA). The FmHA makes direct mortgages to low-income consumers. These mortgages are usually in small towns and rural areas. The requirements for the mortgages depend on the size of the family and income. The interest rate that is charged depends on the borrower's ability to pay. These rates can be very low. The FmHA can guarantee up to 90% of a loan issued by a lender. Many times the FmHA will require the borrower to refinance their mortgage with another lender if their income increases a certain amount. Check with your local FmHA office to find out what the current requirements and income limits for qualification are.

Renegotiated Mortgage

It is also called a rollover mortgage, and is a variation of the balloon mortgage. The interest rate is fixed for a predetermined time, for example, three to five years. After the predetermined time has expired, the interest rate is negotiated. The lender is then obligated to offer refinancing with minimal or no fees, but the borrower can shop around for a more favorable mortgage from other lenders.

Pledged Account Mortgage

A large deposit is paid by the borrower, builder, or any other interested party to the lender at the time of the loan origination. This deposit is invested in an account that will earn interest. The deposit will subsidize the mortgage interest payments in the beginning of the mortgage, which will result in lower payments in the early years. The lender will withdraw an amount every month that is equal to the difference between what the borrower must pay and the actual value of the mortgage at the full interest level. Payments rise gradually over a number of years until they reach their full level, which is the market rate. Then the mortgage becomes a standard ARM or FRM. This type of mortgage could be useful to you if you cannot qualify for a conventional mortgage.

Price-Level Adjusted Mortgage

With this variation of a fixed-rate mortgage, your mortgage payment stays the same in real dollars (adjusted for inflation.) This is how it works: If your mortgage payment is $1,000 and inflation increases 10%, your mortgage payment for the next year also goes up 10% ($1,100). The concept here is that you are repaying the money you borrowed from the lender at its real value. There is a major difference between this and a conventional FRM: The borrower assumes all of the risk for the price level changes, and therefore the lender is willing to lend its money at a lower rate.

Assumable Mortgage

The seller transfers his/her mortgage to the buyer, who then assumes responsibility for the remaining mortgage payments. This is very popular in times of prevailing high interest rates because the buyer assumes the existing mortgage at a lower interest rate than would be possible to obtain at current market rates. The buyer must make a down payment that will cover the difference between the selling price of the home and the balance of the assumable mortgage. The lender must approve this arrangement. Check with your lender to find out if you (the seller) are released from all liability on the original mortgage if the buyer defaults on the loan.

Lease with Option to Buy

After the purchase price, down payment, and monthly payments have been negotiated, the buyer will then make regular rental payments to the seller. A portion of each monthly rental payment will be applied toward the down payment. When enough money has been paid to cover the down payment, the property could then be purchased. Either the seller or financial institution may be the lender. The buyer may forfeit some or all of the money that has been applied to the down payment should he/she cancel the contract.

Shared Appreciation Mortgage

This type of mortgage usually has lower interest rates and thus, lower monthly payments. Here is how it works: The buyer must agree to share with the lender an established amount of the home's appreciation (usually 30% to 50%) after a predetermined number of years, or at the time of sale or transference. The advantage of this type of mortgage is that as the property values rise, the buyer may make a larger profit through the home's appreciation. However, when real estate markets decline, the buyer may be responsible for extra interest payments. A word of caution: If the buyer is unable to pay off the lender's share of the home's value at the agreed-upon time, the buyer would then be forced to either sell the house or refinance.

Equity-Sharing

With this agreement, you have a partner or co-owner who shares the expenses and ownership of the house. For example, you and your sibling might become co-owners in a home. Both parties may share in the appreciation of the property and the tax advantages, as well as any costs incurred. Agreements of this nature must be written by an attorney. There are a number of questions that should be addressed, such as: Can your sibling use his/her share as collateral for another loan? What if you wished to purchase your sibling's share in the future? How would this situation be handled?

Graduated Payment Mortgage (GPM)

With a GPM, monthly payments start at a relatively small amount in the early years of the mortgage. These mortgage payments will increase at a predetermined rate for a certain period of time, most commonly five to ten years. After that period of time, you will pay the regular mortgage payment at a fixed rate of interest. Your mortgage payments will most likely increase between 5% and 8% each year. This approach assumes a person's income will rise over time and that he/she will more easily be able to afford a bigger monthly mortgage payment in the future. A GPM makes a home more affordable in the early years of the mortgage and enables a home buyer to qualify for a bigger house. GPMs usually work best for professionals such as doctors or lawyers who can count on steadily increasing incomes. People in cyclical professions or people who lack job security should probably not get a GPM. GPMs are not very common today; they have been replaced by ARMs.

Growing Equity Mortgage (GEM)

Your equity increases faster with this type of mortgage than with a conventional mortgage. This mortgage has a fixed-rate but your monthly mortgage payments are not the same every year. The interest rate for this mortgage may be below market rates. The mortgage payments continue to increase year after year until the mortgage is paid off. These increases are according to an agreed-upon index or schedule and are applied directly to the principal on the mortgage. The most common increase is 7½%. For example, your mortgage payments in the first year are $1,000, the second year they would increase to $1,075, and the third year they would increase to $1,155. The borrower will save a substantial amount of interest because his/her mortgage will be paid off faster. For example, a 30-year mortgage can be paid off in 15 to 20 years. However, you must be sure your income over the length of the mortgage can keep up with the increased mortgage payments. A GEM should also only be considered by people who are confident their incomes will be steadily increasing over the years. If you get a GEM, make certain that it does not have a prepayment penalty. Such a prepayment penalty could make it very expensive for you to refinance or get out of this mortgage at a later date. GEMS are no longer popular because they, too, have been replaced by ARMs.

Reverse Mortgage

A reverse mortgage is a home loan in which the lender provides the homeowner with access to a sum of money based on the home's equity. The homeowner must have his/her mortgage paid in full or nearly paid off. The minimum age to obtain a reverse mortgage is usually 62. He/she will receive all or part of the equity out of the home in cash while continuing to live in the house. The homeowner has the option to receive a lump sum, establish a line of credit, or receive a certain amount of money each month. The monthly payment can be used to supplement other retirement income. When the house is sold, the lender will receive back the money that has been paid out, which includes principal, interest, and any other costs.

It is important to understand the homeowner is actually borrowing money by reducing the available equity in the house. The amount of money that can be borrowed depends on several factors including the value of the house, interest rates, historical appreciation of real estate in the area, marital status and the age of the homeowner. This money is not considered taxable income and does not affect Social Security or Medicare benefits. All costs should be carefully reviewed, such as interest rates, origination fees, insurance fees for loan guarantees, and closing costs. Costs vary from lender to lender.

Reverse mortgages are not advisable for anyone who expects to stay in their home a short time because of the high up-front costs. Another reason against taking out a reverse mortgage is if you want to leave the home to your heirs. If you have a reverse mortgage and pass away, you will not be leaving your heirs a home free and clear. You will be leaving them a home with a debt.

Property Rights

They consist of the legal free use, enjoyment, and disposal of all a person's acquisitions. For a home buyer to pledge property as collateral for repayment of the mortgage, the borrower must hold legal rights to the property.

Title. Title may be generally defined as the evidence of right which a person has to the possession of property. A lender owes its depositors or investors the assurance that a home buyer or mortgagor has clear title to a property.

Fee Simple Estate. This is absolute title to the property and the owner or borrower can do anything allowed by law to the land: (1) sell it; (2) improve it; or (3) give it away.

Loan-to-Value Ratio (LTV)

The LTV is the mortgage amount divided by the value of the property. The value is determined by the purchase price or appraisal, whichever is lower. On a $100,000 home, if a buyer puts 20% down, the LTV is 80%, which is also the balance of the loan ($80,000). Loans that are considered riskier require lower LTV ratios. Most likely, bare land would require the lowest LTV. For example, many lenders may only lend 40% of the value of bare land. If you want to buy $100,000 of bare land, in this scenario, the lender would only lend you $40,000. To buy it, you would have to come up with $60,000 in cash.

A lender will generally loan between 75% and 90% of the value of a property for the first mortgage, because they are in a safer position. As senior lien holder, the lender will have to be paid off before anyone else. However, the lender will probably require you to purchase private mortgage insurance if the LTV exceeds 80%.

Buydown

A buydown is often used by developers and sometimes by sellers to attract buyers. One type of buydown is when the seller or developer offers the buyer a below-market interest rate (a bought-down rate) to lower the monthly mortgage payment. The developer or seller pays the lender the difference between the official interest rate and the bought-down interest rate. This makes the home more affordable. If two homes for sale are nearly identical and one offers an interest rate buydown, that home will be more likely to sell faster. The interest rate buydown may be temporary or permanent.

Many buydowns last for two to four years, but all buydowns are different and can be negotiated for the number of years, points, and interest rates. Most likely there will be increasing payments during the early years, but no negative amortization will occur.

The buydown may be a subsidy that is opened with some cash and subsidizes the mortgage payment in the early years. At the end of the buydown period, the interest rate returns to the market rate or slightly higher. It may cost the builder $2,000 a year to buydown your interest rate. However, through offering a buydown, the builder may be able to sell a $300,000 home that has been sitting in inventory for several months. Even if he/she has to spend $10,000 during the course of the buydown, the builder can still come out ahead because he/she was able to sell the home more quickly and thus get rid of the carrying costs. Incidentally, some builders may actually raise prices when they offer buydowns, so the buydown does not really cost them anything.

A general rule of thumb is that it is always better to have a buydown with fewer points bought down over a longer period of time. This accomplishes two things: 1) the buyer's income generally increases every year, which will cover the payment after the buydown period, and 2) with fewer points bought down, the buyer does not have monthly payment shock at the end of the buydown period. That is to say, at the end of the buydown period, the buyer's monthly payment will increase by a relatively small percentage, which will easily be affordable, because the buyer's income has increased every year. For this reason, lenders qualify buyers on the bought-down payments, rather than the original higher payments. This allows buyers to buy more of a house for less money before they can truly afford it.

Buydowns are available on FRMs and ARMs and the mortgages are usually for long terms, such as 25 years to 40 years. They generally occupy the safe, senior mortgage position. Because each buydown is different, you will need to evaluate it as it relates to your own situation.

Temporary Buydown. A temporary buydown reduces monthly payment and interest rates during the early years of a mortgage and may be offered by a lender or by a seller. The 3-2-1 buydown is a common form. The interest charged the first year is 3% below the market rate, the interest charged the second year is 2% below the market rate, and the interest charged the third year is 1% below the market rate. In the fourth year, the interest rate returns to market rates or a little higher. Here is an example: If you took out a mortgage when interest rates were 8%, your first year interest rate with a 3-2-1 buydown would be 5%, your second year interest rate would be 6%, your third year interest rate would be 7% and in the fourth year and all remaining years, your interest rate would be 9%.

Permanent Buydown. This will keep the interest rate below market rates for the duration of the mortgage. For example, if FRMs are currently 9%, you may be able to get a buydown at 8% for the length of the mortgage. You might be charged a flat fee or several points of the mortgage amount for this buydown privilege. Permanent buydowns are very expensive because they are in effect for the duration of the mortgage. The lender is taking a substantial risk in offering you this reduced rate mortgage, especially if the lender's cost of funds or interest rates rise. While you may save money on your annual interest with a permanent buydown, you will make up for it by paying a very high fee when you take out this mortgage.

In the Glossary of this book, you will learn additional terms that will be helpful to you in evaluating mortgages and identifying the mortgage that is best for you.

For other sources of information on purchasing a home, call or write:

- Department of Housing and Urban Development. Your phone book will have a local office; and
- Mortgage Bankers Association of America
  1125 15th St. NW, Washington, DC 20005
  (800)793-6222; (202)861-6500.

CHAPTER 3

Eight Myths About Becoming Mortgage Free

Some debts are fun when you are acquiring them, but none are fun when you set about retiring them.

–Ogden Nash

A small debt produces a debtor; a large one, an enemy.

–Publilius Syrus

There are many myths that prevent people from trying to pay off their mortgage quickly. If you believe these myths, they could slow down your progress in eliminating the biggest debt in your life. It is important that I expose these myths to you before they do any more damage. To get the greatest advantage from this book, it is essential that you start with an open mind and that you do not have any misconceptions or erroneous ideas holding you back. Let us look at each of these myths about paying off your mortgage early without making extra payments.

Myth Number 1
Paying Off Your Mortgage Early Only Works for Rich People

Absolutely untrue! Many of my clients are middle-income, working-class people who do not have high incomes, and they are successfully paying off their mortgages in ten years or less, without making extra payments. In fact, some of my clients have lower incomes, and they too are paying off their mortgages early!

Myth Number 2
Paying Off Your Mortgage Early Only Works for People Who Have Small Mortgages

Of course it is easier to pay off small mortgages, however, my strategies work equally well for medium-size and large mortgages. For example, some of my middle-income clients live in expensive homes with large mortgages and they have used my strategies to be in the position to become mortgage free.

If you have a small mortgage and if you use a few of my strategies, you will be able to pay it off exceptionally fast. However, do not be discouraged if you have a large mortgage. It is actually this group of people that my strategies are aimed at and who need to learn them the most. After all, they have the biggest debt and the biggest burden.

Myth Number 3
You Have to Buy Insurance to Become Mortgage Free

This is false. Some people hear about the concept of becoming mortgage free and cynically say, "It is just a trick to get you to buy insurance." While a few of my strategies for becoming mortgage free do involve the use of insurance, the vast majority of them do not. If you decide to use a strategy that does utilize insurance, you may find that you do not have to purchase an additional policy.

Myth Number 4

The Only Way to Pay Off Your Mortgage Early Is with the Biweekly Mortgage Payment Plan or By Making Extra Payments

Absolutely untrue! The biweekly payment plan and making extra payments are certainly two viable options for paying off your mortgage early. However, as you will later learn, they are not the only options, nor are they the best.

Myth Number 5

You Have to Be a Genius at Making Investments To Pay Off Your Mortgage Early

This is incorrect! Some people think that the only way you can pay off your mortgage early is to make a small fortune with your investments and then use that money to pay off your mortgage.

If you are a successful investor, you will be able to pay off your mortgage quickly. However, many people who have investments—such as CDs, bonds, mutual funds, or real estate investments which have earned average returns—are also very successful at paying off their home mortgage early without making extra payments.

Myth Number 6

It Is Too Complicated to Learn How to Pay Off Your Home Mortgage

Nothing could be farther from the truth! The ultimate complication in your life is being tied down to a large mortgage for 15 or 30 years. Paying off your mortgage early is easy by comparison.

Myth Number 7
Paying Off Your Mortgage Early Is All Common Sense

If it were all common sense, then everyone would be doing it. The fact that so few people are paying off their mortgages in ten years or less without extra payments proves that it is not common sense.

Common sense might lead you to figure out one or two of my strategies, yet you still might not know the real advantages and disadvantages of each.

Myth Number 8
It Does Not Make Sense to Become Mortgage Free Because You Lose Your Tax Deduction

Some people do not even investigate becoming mortgage free because they are afraid of losing their mortgage interest tax deduction. This is a big mistake.

The mortgage interest tax deduction is an outstanding tax break. It is one of the last, safe tax deductions left and is almost audit proof for most people. It is understandable why so many people do not want to give up this great tax break. For many Americans, it is the only large tax deduction they have left. If they did not have the mortgage interest deduction, they would be paying more in income taxes.

Although the tax deduction is very important, circumstances can change and there are other factors to consider. You want to be in the position to become mortgage free for three main reasons: (1) tax deductions can be eliminated; (2) your financial situation does not allow you to take advantage of the mortgage interest deduction; and (3) you may not want a mortgage due to health problems, financial difficulties, limited retirement income, or the psychological benefits, such as peace of mind in not having a mortgage.

These are the eight myths that prevent people from becoming mortgage free. Do not let them hold you back.

CHAPTER

4

Ten Mortgage Misconceptions

A man in debt is so far a slave.

–Ralph Waldo Emerson, *Conduct of Life: Wealth*

If you would know the value of money, go try to borrow some; for he that goes a-borrowing goes a-sorrowing.

–Benjamin Franklin, *Poor Richard's Almanac*

Every day, across the United States, thousands of people apply for mortgages. A young couple is buying their first home, a businessman is buying a larger house, a single working woman is buying a townhouse, an investor is buying another apartment building, and a retired couple is buying a second home in Florida.

Each of these people have probably sought advice. Some have asked for advice from other home buyers, family members, friends, coworkers, neighbors, accountants, attorneys, bankers, financial planners, and mortgage lenders. The advice they have received has been well-intentioned, and yet it has probably also been biased, confusing, and contradictory. A home purchase is probably the biggest investment most people will ever make. Both the purchase of the home and the acquisition of the mortgage deserve serious attention and respect.

As educated and well-intentioned as many people are, they often make serious mistakes when getting a mortgage. Many of these mistakes can be traced to underlying misconceptions. These misconceptions can cost borrowers tens of thousands or hundreds of thousands of dollars over the duration of a mortgage. Saddest of all, many borrowers lose all this money without ever knowing there were alternatives which could have saved them this money. In this chapter, I will teach you ten mortgage misconceptions and will show you how not to fall victim to them.

Mortgage Misconception Number 1
Believing That Choosing a Home and Choosing a Mortgage Are Logical Decisions

You may fool yourself into believing that buying a house is made through logical analysis and based on sound money principles. The reality is that no matter what type of house you bought or the type of mortgage you obtained, your decision was probably based on emotions.

For example, after buying a house, one of my clients said to me, "Sure, I was emotional. The minute I saw the house, I knew it was for me. I was proud that I could afford it and I couldn't wait to tell my family and friends. I wanted to show it off and park my sports car in the driveway. Yeah, the house had some minor flaws that I didn't notice in my excitement—you know, love is blind—but eventually I'll fix them." I noticed that my client seemed anxious as he was speaking to me. These "minor flaws" that he did not notice eventually cost him $8,700 to fix!

To overcome false information in buying a house or getting a mortgage is to admit to yourself that both activities are emotional processes and that you will be emotional. Be honest with yourself, be aware of your emotions, and pay attention to the things that you say to yourself. For example, when you start saying, "I have to have this, I just have to have this!" Slow down. The more you tell yourself, "I have to have this house," the more likely you will be to overpay for it because you are being controlled by your emotions and you may not negotiate the best price.

There are a number of steps you can take in choosing the right house and choosing the right mortgage. Let us review some of them. First, remind yourself that you are looking for a place to live. You are not looking for something to impress all of your friends. If the house impresses your friends that is fine, but it should not be a major reason you buy it.

Second, do not rush out and buy a house just because you had a fight with your landlord. Believe it or not, this can be a motivating factor in some people's decision to buy a house. There is nothing wrong with wanting to get a home of your own. In fact, it could be a financially sound decision. However, make sure that you do it for the right reasons and make sure you do your homework.

Third, buying a home and getting a mortgage should be viewed as a serious, long-term commitment. You do not want to rush into buying a home or getting a mortgage.

Fourth, do not buy a home because your parents, in-laws, brother, sister, or friend told you that you should. This should be your decision or a decision made with your spouse. If you are buying a home to please someone other than yourself, you may never be happy living in it. Do not buy a particular home to fulfill someone else's dream. You need to do it because of your own internal motivations.

Fifth, do not buy a house just because it is a family tradition. Do not feel pressured to buy a home in a certain neighborhood because all of your family lives in that neighborhood.

Sixth, do not buy a house in a remote area just because you want to "get away from it all," unless you are sure you will be happy. Just because you hate the smog and congestion of the city does not mean you will be happy in the suburbs. Ask yourself these questions: What will I do with my free evenings? How far will I have to drive to get to the grocery store or the movie theater? What are the schools like? Will my children get a good education? What services are offered by the suburb? How far am I from the hospital and doctor? and How many hours a week will I have to spend driving to and from work?

In addition to liking your house, you also have to like the mortgage you have. Many people have made the mistake of getting a mortgage that was tied to an index they did not understand or an index that was highly volatile. As interest rates move up, some indexes move up slowly and others quickly. If you have one that quickly goes up, you might get discouraged by the rapidly rising interest rate on your mortgage.

One of the most important points that I have learned in all of my years of working as a financial planner is that mortgages are also emotional. Having a mortgage that is not the best for your financial situation, such as a high-interest rate, a large prepayment penalty, or high monthly payments, can be a very negative experience and can discourage people from using their mortgage to its fullest advantage. Get a mortgage that you will be happy with and comfortable with for many years. You will feel good as you pay it down and pay it off.

In my opinion, one of the biggest mistakes lenders make is that they do not talk to borrowers about the emotional aspects of getting a mortgage. It is more than a logical process, or a process of objectively comparing numbers. If it were a logical process, then a computer could select a mortgage for you. Mortgages are even emotional for lenders. Their own emotions, prejudices, and biases may lead them to steer you toward one mortgage and away from another one.

The emotional aspect of mortgages is one of the most overlooked of all factors that could influence your decision as to whether or not you will want to pay off your mortgage early. I have read many books on mortgages and I have never seen this extremely important topic covered in any other book. Unless you understand the emotions involved in getting a mortgage, you may end up with the wrong type of mortgage.

Mortgage Misconception Number 2
You Should Focus Primarily on "What You Can Afford to Pay Each Month"

There is nothing wrong with focusing on how much you can afford to pay on your mortgage each month. In fact, this factor must be considered. However, there is an over-emphasis on this one factor and it leads many people to give less thought to other important factors. Some people think that once they have determined how much they can pay each month, they will then know how much house they can afford and what kind of mortgage to get. Why, you may ask, is this thinking erroneous?

First, how much you can afford changes over time. To intelligently answer this question, you must review your past and current financial situation and project where you will be in the future. You should also develop a plan if something happens to you, such as being laid-off or fired from work, becoming ill, dying, losing your business, or other financial difficulties.

Second, you should look at how much insurance you have. If you get into an accident or become seriously ill, how much—if anything—will you be able to count on from disability insurance? What if one of your children becomes ill? Do you have adequate health insurance for your entire family? Will you be able to maintain your current lifestyle?

What if your spouse becomes seriously ill or gets in an accident? Do you need two incomes to maintain your lifestyle and to pay your mortgage? If you get laid off from work or if you are fired, will you easily be able to find a new job? Will you be able to make as much money? Will you have to move? You should also ask yourself, "How much do I have in savings?" and "Will that be enough to help me pay my mortgage for several months or a year if something happens to me or my job?"

All of these factors must be considered when determining how much you want to spend on a house and how large a mortgage you can afford. Unfortunately, there are some lenders who do not take enough time to review your current finances in determining how much you can afford. If you want to do a deeper analysis, you will have to do it yourself, or see a qualified financial planner.

In determining how much they can afford, some people err on the side of estimating too little and others on the side of estimating too much. If you do not care how accurate your estimate is, you should not even waste your time and energy to do this exercise. The figure you arrive at is only useful to the degree that it is accurate. The more accurate it is, the more useful it will be to you. Remember also that you want to have a realistic figure of how much you can afford now, next year, in five years, and even in ten years.

It is obvious how people can overestimate how much they can afford. Millions of people have done this. People who worked in the oil and gas industry made this mistake just before the crash in oil prices in the early 1980s which resulted in thousands of foreclosures in the oil-patch states. People working in the aerospace industry and the defense industry overestimated how much they could afford and they paid the price when thousands of people were laid off as these industries were forced to cut back after the Cold War ended. As

Detroit began laying off its highly paid labor force and began using more and more machines, high school graduates who thought they had a $28 an hour job for life were suddenly unemployed. Unfortunately, many of them also found they could no longer afford the houses they had purchased.

How can you plan for the future? How can you know if your job is safe and secure? There are almost always warning signs that changes are taking place in our economy. For example, for many years automobile workers noticed that the plants they were working in were adding machines to the assembly lines. They noticed that Japanese and other foreign car manufacturers were controlling an increasingly larger percentage of the United States automobile market. In fact, all they had to do was look in the General Motors and Ford parking lots to see many of their own employees were driving foreign cars. There were also articles in the newspaper stating that automobile manufacturers were relocating to lower-income states. Similarly, in the 1980s there were many warning signs that the aerospace and defense industries would continue to cut back costs and that oil prices were headed still lower. Today, you can see there is incredible pressure on the health care industry to reduce costs.

However, if you are one of the fortunate few in a high-income profession, if you own a business that is highly profitable, or if your investments are doing extremely well, you do not want to buy a smaller house than you want or need. Some people look only at their current income and decide to settle for a smaller house than they want. If they had analyzed their future income, they might very well buy the house they really want and need today.

It is costly, both in terms of time and money, to buy a smaller house than you need today. Moving is expensive and time consuming. Why buy a small house, or a house in a neighborhood you would prefer not to live in if you can afford a house you want in a neighborhood you like? If you accurately analyze your income, savings, and investments and see that there is a strong possibility that you will be making much more money in a few years, why not buy the house you want?

There is still another reason to buy that larger house today. For many Americans, the home mortgage interest deduction is the only tax deduction left. Why not get a larger tax deduction? Why not let the government help subsidize your purchase of a nicer, bigger, more luxurious home for you and your family?

Because people do not systematically and objectively analyze their probable future income, savings, and investments for emergencies, they almost always make serious mistakes when they arrive at a figure estimating how much house they can afford. In some cases, these figures are so inaccurate, they are worthless. Do not let this happen to you. Do not let a lender or a real estate agent tell you that you can afford a mortgage that is "28% of your income" if you know your income is likely to significantly go up or down in the future year(s). Do your own thorough, objective analysis of how much you will be able to afford today, in three years, in five years, and in ten years, or seek advice from a financial planner. Thus, when you get a mortgage, it will be one you are truly comfortable with and one you will find easy to quickly pay off!

Mortgage Misconception Number 3
The Best Mortgage Is the One With the Lowest Interest Rate

If you ask most people which kind of mortgage is the best, they probably would say, "The one with the lowest interest rate."

To really find out which mortgage is the best, you need to study many other variables besides the interest rate. For example, What are the fees? or How quickly can the mortgage be approved? In some cases, you may need rapid mortgage approval. A client of mine saved $30,000 on an apartment building because he was able to obtain very rapid mortgage funding. Even if he had to pay a slightly higher interest rate for this mortgage, it was well worth it. In some cases, a homeowner may not even sell you a home unless you can commit to rapid financing.

Another variable that should be studied are indexes. An index can have a tremendous impact on how much you pay on your mortgage. For example, a client of mine secured a mortgage using the prime rate index. When he got the mortgage, the prime rate was 6½%. Mortgages using other indexes were available at that time that had an interest rate of 7% to 8%. He thought he was doing very well. However, he ignored the fact that the prime rate can be a notoriously volatile index because the prime rate is subject to daily change. Within a few years, the prime rate shot up to 10%. Friends of his who had mortgages with more stable indexes, such as the Federal Home Loan Bank index, were still paying only 8%. Since he focused only on the prime rate's low initial interest rate and because he ignored the volatility of this index, he is now paying more than $200 extra per month on his mortgage.

Points can also have a tremendous impact on what you actually pay on a mortgage, especially if you end up refinancing or selling your home. Many low interest rate mortgages have very high points. If the lender gives you a break on the interest rate, they make up for it by collecting money from you in the form of points. I have seen very low interest rate mortgages that charge five points. The following is an example that explains what could happen if you refinance or sell your home with such a mortgage.

Let us assume you are acquiring a $100,000 mortgage at 6% interest. To get this low interest rate mortgage, you pay four points up front, which is $4,000. At the end of one year, you have paid $6,000 in interest. What happens if you are transferred or laid off from work and have to sell your home? What happens if you get sick or you are in an accident and have to sell your home? What happens if you want to sell your home to trade up or trade down? If you sell your home in one year, you have paid $10,000 (interest costs of $6,000 and points of $4,000). Also, your out-of-pocket expenses are much higher because you probably had to pay various fees, such as closing costs, title fees, transfer fees, document fees, and appraisal fees.

If you only paid $10,000, the effective annual interest rate you paid was 10%. If the market interest rate was 7%, you lost $3,000 by taking out a *low-interest rate* mortgage. If the market interest rate was 8%, you still lost $2,000.

What if you had to pay off the mortgage, sell your house, or refinance after two years? You would have paid $12,000 in interest (let us assume in year two you also paid $6,000 in interest) and the $4,000 in points for a total of $16,000 in costs. This is the equivalent of paying 8% annual interest. If you had to sell or refinance at the end of three years, your total costs would be $22,000 for an equivalent annualized cost of slightly more than 7%. If market rates were 7%, you would still be behind after three years. If you pay high points to get a *low-interest rate mortgage*, it could take three years or longer for you just to catch up to where you would have been if you had simply obtained a mortgage with low points and a higher interest rate.

On average, Americans move every seven years. Many Americans move before they have been in a house seven years. If you are someone who moves frequently or sooner than you had anticipated, by obtaining a *low-interest rate* mortgage with *high points* you could lose money.

Another characteristic of *low-interest rate mortgages* to be aware of is prepayment penalties. Some lenders may grant *low-interest rate mortgages* because they know the mortgages will be highly profitable to them after a certain period of time. To discourage you from refinancing or paying off your mortgage early, they establish prepayment penalties. If the mortgage is refinanced or prepaid before a certain date, you will be penalized by having to pay extra interest. The prepayment penalty will not apply if you sell your house. Try adding six months extra interest to a mortgage you have only been paying on for two years. You will find that your effective annualized interest rate is more for this *low-interest rate mortgage* than it would have been if you had taken out a higher interest rate mortgage. However, most mortgages today do not have prepayment penalties. Check with your own lender.

It is important to understand what the caps are on the ARM you are applying for. You need to know what the caps will be per adjustment period, for example, the range can be 2% per adjustment period and 6% maximum over the life of the mortgage. You should compare the caps with several lenders.

Finally, a very significant consideration is to obtain a mortgage that will give you the maximum tax deductions, which in return will save you income taxes. Obtaining a mortgage with the lowest interest rate may not be the best mortgage. You should consider all of the other variables that were discussed.

Mortgage Misconception Number 4

All Lenders Have the Same Costs and Fees

You should meet with several lenders to compare costs and fees because they vary from lender to lender. Lenders are in the business of lending money. Because of competition, you may be able to negotiate these costs and fees. Many of you spend the majority of your time and effort looking for a house and negotiating the price. As a result, you have little energy left to meet with several lenders, which puts you in a very vulnerable position. Since you just want to get everything over with, you do not shop for a mortgage or compare costs. Making a quick decision can be a very costly mistake. A little effort spent comparison shopping could save you a substantial amount of money in total mortgage charges.

Mortgage Misconception Number 5
I Have Received the Best Advice

Borrowers are often under the misconception that their mortgage lenders, certified public accountants, attorneys, financial planners, friends, relatives, and neighbors have given them the very best financial advice. This is sometimes not true!

When you ask someone else for advice or when they freely volunteer advice to you about what kind of mortgage you should get, ask yourself this question: Is this person really an expert on 15-year versus 30-year mortgages? Are they really up to date on all the advantages and disadvantages of fixed-rate mortgages versus adjustable-rate mortgages? Do they know the benefits and drawbacks of VA and FHA mortgages? Are they really an expert on mortgage points and origination fees? Is this person prejudiced or biased toward the products his/her lending institution is offering?

Also ask yourself if this person has done first-hand research him/herself or if he/she is just repeating a cliché. Finally, ask yourself if this person has the best mortgage him/herself? Is this person rapidly paying down his/her own mortgage? If not, then why should you take his/her advice? I have one important rule in financial planning: Do not take financial advice from people who are not experts in this field.

You have to work hard to earn money. Do not spend your money on a mortgage unless it is the best for your personal situation. Do not take advice that could lead you to pay much more than you have to on your home mortgage.

The more knowledge you have about mortgages and how to pay them off, the more money you will save and the faster you will become mortgage free. There are many qualified financial planners who can help you to obtain the best mortgage advice.

Mortgage Misconception Number 6

Making Extra Payments Is a Great Idea

A mortgage is one of the cheapest loans you will ever take out in your life, plus it is tax deductible. It is important to know that each time you make an extra payment on your mortgage, you lose that valuable tax deduction. If you make enough extra payments, you could easily lose half or even more of your tax deductions.

If your mortgage is at 8% and you are in the 25% tax bracket, your net cost for the money is only 6%. Why prepay your mortgage that has a net cost of only 6% and lose the best tax deduction you will ever have? There are many mutual funds that have averaged better than 6%. You can also earn more than 6% by investing in quality real estate. Since 1929 the stock market has averaged more than a 9% rate of return. A qualified financial planner or stock broker can help you earn a rate of return that is higher than 6% on your investments.

Even though making extra payments will reduce the outstanding principal balance and will save interest on the mortgage, you forfeit the option to invest the extra payments in an alternative investment with a higher rate of return. You will learn more about this concept in Chapter 11. As you can see, it is often a misconception that making extra payments is a great idea.

Mortgage Misconception Number 7

Shorter Term Mortgages Are Better Mortgages

Recently, 15-year mortgages have become very popular. Many people have come to the conclusion that they do not want to spend 30 years paying off their mortgage. Even though their intentions are good, getting a 15-year mortgage may not be the best option. Here are two reasons why.

First, 15-year mortgages have higher monthly payments. This means that you cannot afford as large of a house if you get a 15-year mortgage. In addition, you have to use more of your spendable income each month to pay off that mortgage. If you should get sick or are temporarily laid off from work, you might find you cannot manage these high monthly payments. Many people have lost their home to foreclosure because they could not afford the high monthly payments of a 15-year mortgage.

Second, your mortgage tax deduction rapidly disappears on a 15-year mortgage. This means that the government gets more and more of your income. You have less income after taxes and you have to spend more of it on your mortgage. Do you really want to be in this position? Chapter 8, The Mortgage Controversy: 15-Year Versus 30-Year Mortgages, discusses in detail the reasons why you may want to avoid a 15-year mortgage.

Mortgage Misconception Number 8

Everyone Should Pay Off Their Home Mortgages

The title of my book is *How to Become Mortgage Free in Ten Years or Less, Without Extra Payments*. You might, therefore, think that I advise everyone to pay off their home mortgages early. That is false. Believe it or not, there are some very good reasons to have a home mortgage. As previously mentioned, it provides one of the best, nearly audit-proof tax deductions and is probably the cheapest loan you can obtain.

If you have other good uses for your money, you might want to invest it elsewhere rather than in your house. After all, if you can make 20% on your money by investing it in your business, or 10% in the stock market or other real estate, why put it in your home?

Mortgage Misconception Number 9

All Adjustable-Rate Mortgages Are the Same

It surprises me how many people believe that all adjustable-rate mortgages are the same. I have actually had intelligent, well-educated people come into my office and tell me, "Sandy, I've looked at several different mortgages and they pretty much average out. Some have lower interest rates, but they have higher fees. Some have lower fees, but they have higher points. It's all about the same. It doesn't matter what I get."

It *does* matter what you get! Adjustable-rate mortgages are vastly different. A small difference of one-half of 1% in an interest rate can add up to several thousand dollars over the duration of your mortgage. For example, on a $150,000, 30-year mortgage at 8% interest you would have paid total interest of $246,233; at 8½% total interest paid would have been $265,213; and at 9% you would have paid $284,495 in total interest, assuming interest rates remained level. The choice of one index over another in an adjustable-rate mortgage can cost you tens of thousands of dollars over the duration of the mortgage, even if both indexes start out exactly the same!

Do not get discouraged and say, "It isn't worth it to compare." Even if a lender or a friend tells you, "All adjustable-rate mortgages are pretty much the same," don't believe them. Making this assumption could cost you a great deal of money. By comparing the differences between adjustable-rate mortgages you could save enough money to buy a new car, remodel your kitchen, pay for a vacation, provide additional money for retirement, or best of all, pay off your mortgage early.

Furthermore, do not assume that fixed-rate mortgages are all the same. Fixed-rate mortgages have different interest rates, fees, prepayment penalties, points, and many other differing characteristics. Study the details. Knowing the advantages and disadvantages of each mortgage can save you a lot of hard-earned money.

Mortgage Misconception Number 10
Your Private Mortgage Insurance (PMI) Will Automatically Drop from Your Mortgage Payments

Do not wait for your lender to give you an invitation to drop your private mortgage insurance (PMI). PMI generates revenue for lenders, and many do not want to forfeit this income. Therefore, inquire as to whether or not you can drop your PMI or when you qualify to drop your PMI.

PMI is usually required if you take out a mortgage with less than 20% down payment. When you have a minimum of 20% equity in your house and made your mortgage payments on time you may qualify to drop your PMI. The 20% equity can be reached because your house has appreciated in value and by paying down your mortgage principal.

If your mortgage was bought by the Federal National Mortgage Association (Fannie Mae) or the Federal Home Loan Mortgage Corporation (Freddie Mac), which buy mortgages from lenders, you have a very good chance of qualifying because both organizations require that lenders agree to drop PMI if a mortgage holder meets their requirements.

Call, write, or fax a letter to your lender inquiring about having your PMI dropped. Ask your lender what the requirements are for dropping your PMI. It is definitely worth asking about. If your PMI is dropped, your monthly mortgage payments will be reduced.

Conclusion

You have now learned and been warned about ten mortgage misconceptions that collectively cost Americans millions of dollars each year. Do not let any of these misconceptions affect you. Use the knowledge you have acquired so far from reading this book and the knowledge you will acquire from the remainder of this book to get the mortgage that is most ideal for your unique financial situation.

CHAPTER

5

The Best Time To Refinance Your Mortgage

Creditors have better memories than debtors.

–Benjamin Franklin, *Poor Richard's Almanac*

Lend less then thou owest.

–Shakespeare, *King Lear*

One of the best reasons to refinance is to profit from falling interest rates. Doing so might enable you to save thousands of dollars in interest charges and to have more money available that you can use for other important things (such as college tuition). For example, let us say you have a $100,000 mortgage at 10% interest. Your current annual interest expenditure is $10,000. If interest rates fall to 8% and you refinance your mortgage at that rate, you will save $2,000 for the year ($8,000 current interest). This may not seem like a lot at first, but over several years this can amount to a great deal of money. If your mortgage is more than $100,000, you will save even more.

You can also use lower interest rates and refinancing to shorten the life of your mortgage. You might save enough money by refinancing at a lower interest rate to reduce your 30-year mortgage to a 20-year mortgage. To accomplish this, you would want to continue making the same monthly payments you were making before you refinanced. The extra money you would be paying into your mortgage each month would go directly toward paying down your principal. Since you were already accustomed to making this payment, it would not feel like an extra cash outlay for you. This is a relatively easy way to rapidly pay down your mortgage when interest rates fall. This one strategy can help you quickly reduce the size of the principal amount owed. If you combine it with strategies you will learn in Chapter 12, you will be able to pay down your mortgage (and to completely pay it off) even more quickly.

To avoid losing your tax deductions by making these extra payments, you could invest the money instead. Either way you would have benefited by refinancing your mortgage at a lower interest rate.

Considering all of these benefits, you may be wondering why more people are not refinancing their homes when interest rates drop. Some people believe it is "too much work." They remember how difficult and time consuming it was to get their original mortgage and they do not want to go through such a long and drawn-out process again. What you need to understand is that refinancing your mortgage when interest rates decline is often easier than getting your original mortgage. If you have made all your mortgage payments on time and if you are making as much money or more money than you made when you obtained your original mortgage, refinancing should be an easy process.

Let me explain why refinancing is easy. Let us assume that home prices have stayed level or have increased in your community. Also, you have been building up equity with every mortgage payment. This increased equity in your home makes your new, lower interest mortgage even less risky for your lender. If you have been able to afford the monthly payments at the higher interest rate, you should definitely be able to pay the new mortgage payments at the lower interest rate. For this reason, lenders are prone to approve such refinancings even more rapidly than they approve new mortgages.

In addition, the paperwork for refinancing your existing mortgage is often less involved than the process for a new mortgage. For example, your lender may not have to do a full appraisal on your property. Of course, there are various factors that the lender will need to consider, such as, Have you made your mortgage payments on time? Do you have good credit? and Does your home have any liens against it?

If home prices have fallen in your community or if you are not making as much money as you previously made, then refinancing might take a little more time; however, it will still be worth it. You may be able to get a new mortgage that could save you between \$2,000 and \$10,000 or even more every year by reducing your interest expense.

Besides saving money through lower interest rates, another major reason people refinance their mortgage is to obtain a lump sum of cash. However, you should ask yourself if taking out a lump sum of money is really the best use of your home's equity. Make certain that you have a valid reason for taking any money out of your home.

Deciding Whether or Not to Refinance

Now that you understand that refinancing can benefit you by reducing your interest rate, lowering your monthly payments, increasing your cash flow, shortening your mortgage term, and by giving you access to a lump sum of cash, should you refinance? Whether or not you should refinance depends on a variety of factors and one of the most important of these is how much interest rates have fallen.

The generally accepted rule of thumb is that if interest rates have fallen by 2%, it makes sense to refinance. Bear in mind that interest rates do not have to fall by 2% for you to profit from refinancing. Like all rules of thumb this one is not perfect. It might make sense for you to refinance if interest rates drop by only 1%. On the other hand, it might not make sense for you to refinance even if interest rates drop by 3%. Therefore, you must ask yourself this question, "What would make it worthwhile for me to refinance?" The answer: You must look at your total costs of refinancing, such as the origination costs and closing costs you pay for the new mortgage which could have a dramatic impact on the effective interest rate you pay.

Let us first look at a best-case scenario. There are some lenders who offer *no cost* mortgages so they can keep your business. This means that you pay nothing for the new appraisal, you pay nothing for a credit report, for documentation fees, or loan processing fees. The lender absorbs all of those costs. The lender can make a profit by selling your mortgage at a higher interest rate to an investor. If you can get such a true *no cost* mortgage, it might make sense to refinance even if you could save just 1/2 of 1% per year. If you can lower your interest rate from 8% to 7 1/2%, why not refinance? The key is that you have to make absolutely certain there are no costs associated with the new mortgage if the interest rate reduction is small.

If the total costs are high, refinancing may not make sense even if you can get a 3% or greater interest rate reduction. For example, some lenders may charge 4% or more of the amount borrowed in fees. If you borrow $200,000, you might have to pay $8,000 or more in fees to get the new mortgage. Even if you can lower your interest rate by 3%, it could take years just to break even.

If you sold your home before the break-even point, you would actually lose money by taking out this new lower interest rate mortgage. Therefore, you should never consider a high-cost or high-points refinancing unless you are certain you will stay in your home for at least the period of time it takes to recover the expense of the new mortgage through your interest savings.

Another important factor to consider is how you will pay for the cost of refinancing. If you have the money and if you have no better use for it, then it may make sense to go ahead and pay cash for the refinancing even if the fees are somewhat high—assuming of course, that you can get a substantial reduction in your interest rate. However, many lenders will allow you to add the points and fees on to your mortgage balance.

I recommend that you never add the points and fees on to your mortgage balance unless these costs are extremely low and/or you have absolutely no other source of funds. Why is this so important? Let us say you have to pay 4% in fees and points. On a $200,000 mortgage, this means an additional $8,000 would be added to your mortgage balance. Instead of having to pay back $200,000, you will have to pay back $208,000. You will be paying interest on the additional $8,000. However, the additional interest charges are tax deductible.

Remember that in the early years of your mortgage very little of your monthly payment goes toward principal reduction. Almost all of your monthly payment goes toward interest. If $8,000 extra is added to your unpaid balance—depending on your interest rate—it could take four years or even longer to pay off these fees and points and reduce the mortgage principal to the original amount. For this reason, I urge extreme caution in allowing any fees or points to be added to your mortgage balance when you refinance. The only exception is to add the fees or points to your mortgage if you can invest the money where it will earn a greater return than what the lender is charging you.

Another factor to keep in mind when you refinance is that you are paying some of the fees for the second time. You paid most of these fees (for example, appraisal, credit check, title search) once when you took out your original mortgage. Why pay them again? You must truly be saving a significant amount of money to justify repaying these fees.

Here is a great money-saving idea: Negotiate a reduction in these fees when you refinance your mortgage. If you are staying with the same lender and if you have a good payment history with that lender, they may reduce the fees. In addition, if you obtained your first mortgage relatively recently from that lender they might also be agreeable to further reductions in fees. It might not be necessary to resubmit all the paperwork. Finally, if home prices have appreciated enough in your neighborhood or if you have significantly paid down your mortgage, you might have sufficient equity that it might not be necessary to do a full appraisal. This could save you time and money.

I have known some people who refinanced their homes three times in less than ten years. Even if you get a sufficient reduction in interest rates each time you refinance, the costs and fees of refinancing will reduce your actual savings. The low interest rate should not be the only criteria to consider. Look at your total costs—your total savings minus your total expenses—before making a decision as to whether or not it is beneficial for you to refinance. Do not forget to factor in the lost future earnings* principle on your money, which will be explained in Chapter 9.

---

* *Lost future earnings* and *loss of future earnings* are interchangeable. In this book, we will use lost future earnings.

In addition, remember to carefully consider how long you will be staying in your current home. Will you be living in that home long enough to recover the costs to refinance? Are you absolutely certain? Talk with your employer. Is there a possibility you may be transferred? Is your company opening a plant or an office in a new area? Is there a chance your spouse might be transferred? What if you have another child in the next few years? Is there a possibility you might need to move to a bigger home, or to a neighborhood with better schools? Do you have an elderly parent who might need you to move closer so that you can take care of him or her? If it is likely that you might be moving in the next few years—before you can recapture the costs of the refinance—you may not want to apply for the new mortgage.

The Tax Implications of Refinancing

In this section, I will give you an idea of what some of the most important tax implications of refinancing are at the time this book is being written. Tax laws are complex and constantly changing. You should check with your tax advisor and financial planner for clarification on these two points: (1) to learn exactly how much of your mortgage interest is tax deductible, such as the phase-out rules for exemptions and itemized deductions for high-income earners; and (2) to learn all of your options to refinance and which one is the best course of action for you to take.

Currently, you can deduct interest on a home mortgage only up to an amount that equals the original mortgage balance plus the cost of any home improvements. You are also allowed to deduct interest on any home equity loan up to $100,000. Let us say your original mortgage is $100,000 and you made $100,000 in improvements. You also have a $100,000 home equity loan. According to current tax law, in this example, you can only deduct interest on loans of

$300,000 ($100,000 original mortgage plus $100,000 cost of improvements plus $100,000 home equity loan).

Remember also that the maximum amount of mortgage interest you can deduct on your principal residence and a second home is limited to the interest on $1,000,000 in indebtedness. You are also allowed $100,000 on a home equity loan. The total mortgage interest (including home equity loans) that is tax deductible is $1,100,000. Interest on any amount above this is not tax deductible.

There is one more restriction you need to be aware of: The combined total of your original mortgage and home equity loan cannot exceed the fair market value of the residence. If your home is worth $250,000 and you have $300,000 in loans against it, the interest on $50,000 of that loan is not tax deductible.

How could you end up with loans on the house that are in excess of its true market value? Unfortunately, if real estate prices have fallen dramatically, you could find yourself in this situation. For example, there were people in certain parts of the country who paid $400,000 for homes and obtained $300,000 mortgages against them. Some of these homes declined in value to $250,000 or even less. Homeowners who were left with $300,000 in mortgages found they could deduct the interest on only the first $250,000—the fair market value—of those homes.

Exceptions to the Tax Deduction Rules On Refinancings

There is a strategy that actually enables you to convert nondeductible interest from your mortgage into tax-deductible interest. If you use the money you have borrowed against your home for investment purposes, the interest on that loan may be tax deductible. Consult your tax advisor. The following example will show you how you can use this to your advantage.

Assume that the amount of your original mortgage is $100,000 and that you made no improvements to your home. Normally, your tax deductible interest would be limited to a loan amount of $200,000—$100,000 original mortgage plus $100,000 home equity loan—regardless of how much your home has appreciated. Let us say you already had a $200,000 loan and your lender was willing to lend you an additional $100,000. If you did borrow that $100,000 and if you used it for investment purposes (to buy stocks or mutual funds, for example) the interest on that additional $100,000 debt would be tax deductible.

You would deduct the interest on the first $200,000 as **mortgage** debt and deduct the interest on the last $100,000 as **investment** debt. The only exception is a limitation that states you cannot claim a tax deduction on the interest from a mortgage taken out to buy tax-exempt bonds or a single premium whole life insurance policy. Therefore, if you used the $100,000 in additional debt to buy tax-free municipal bonds you could not deduct the interest on that debt. However, if you used the $100,000 to buy stocks, corporate bonds, or mutual funds, the interest on that debt would be fully tax deductible. Keep in mind that the earnings on your investments would be taxable. Knowing about this exception to the tax deductibility limitations on refinanced mortgages and home equity loans and how to use it can benefit you tremendously. I recommend that you consult with your tax advisor to learn the latest laws or any changes in the rules concerning this exception.

Be Aware of Prepayment Penalties

The value of your home has risen substantially. Your credit is excellent. Interest rates have fallen. It is a perfect time to refinance your mortgage and/or take out some equity.

You submit an application for a new mortgage that will give you $100,000 cash from the equity in your home. The lender is ready to approve the new mortgage and to pay off your old mortgage when someone discovers that your old mortgage has a prepayment penalty. You are now faced with paying thousands of dollars in the form of a prepayment penalty to get rid of that old mortgage.

What should you do? Should you forget about refinancing? Should you just give up and pay the prepayment penalty? There are several points I would like to address about mortgage prepayment penalties.

First, before you even apply for a new mortgage, read the documentation for your current mortgage. Is there a prepayment penalty? You never want to be surprised to learn about this penalty just days before you are scheduled to close on a new mortgage. If there is no prepayment penalty you have nothing to worry about. Also, your current lender cannot add a prepayment penalty after your mortgage has been approved.

Second, even if you are refinancing with another lender, you should ask your existing lender about waiving or reducing the prepayment penalty. They may be willing to do this if you are a good customer who has other accounts with them.

Third, what if your lender will not waive or reduce the prepayment penalty? Almost all prepayment penalties have time limitations, many last only for two or three years. The longest I have seen is five years. If you have been living in your home for three years and the prepayment penalty only lasts for two years, you no longer have a prepayment penalty. If your prepayment penalty lasts for four years and you have been living in your home for three years and ten months, you only have two months left. You can start the process of getting a new mortgage now. Tell your new lender about the prepayment penalty and schedule the closing of your mortgage for one day after the prepayment penalty expires.

Fourth, in many cases, prepayment penalties decline as the years go by. For example, if you refinance during the first year of your mortgage, the prepayment penalty might be 2% of the mortgage amount. If you refinance during the second year of your mortgage, the prepayment penalty might be 1% of the mortgage amount. If you refinance during the third year of your mortgage, the prepayment penalty might only be 1/2 of 1%. Let us say you are in the third year of your mortgage and are very motivated to refinance. You may decide that paying 1/2 of 1% is worth it to refinance now.

Finally, if you find yourself with a very high prepayment penalty, you have one additional option. Instead of refinancing your existing first mortgage, it might make more sense to simply take out a home equity loan. Taking out a home equity loan does not incur any type of prepayment penalty.

If you do have to pay a prepayment penalty, the fee you pay could be tax deductible. According to current tax laws, prepayment penalties can be included as home mortgage interest on your tax forms. I recommend that you check with your tax advisor regarding the latest tax laws.

There are about 12 states that do not allow prepayment penalties. Some states have no restrictions, while others have limitations. You should find out what the prepayment laws are in your state.

Determining Your Break-Even Point

Once you have done everything you can to minimize your fees, costs, and expenses, you need to add up what your total costs for the refinancing will be. If those fees are excessively high and if it will take you a long time to reach the break-even point, it may not be in your best interest to refinance your mortgage—unless you are certain you will be living in your home for many years.

The length of time it takes you to recapture the costs of refinancing is a crucial factor to consider. Until you recover those expenses, you have not saved any money by refinancing your home.

It is relatively simple to figure your break-even point when you refinance a mortgage. First, determine your total refinancing costs (for example, all points, fees, charges). Let us assume your total refinancing costs were $4,100. Next, determine what your monthly savings will be from obtaining this new lower interest rate mortgage. For example, if your old monthly mortgage payment was $996 and your new monthly mortgage payment is $907, your monthly savings will be $89.

Finally, to learn your break-even point, divide your total refinancing costs ($4,100) by your monthly savings ($89). Doing so tells you that your break-even point is 46.06 months. It will take you 46 months, almost four years, to break even on this refinance. You will not save any money until you have had this new mortgage for almost four years. After 46 months, you will begin saving $89 a month. If there is a good possibility you may move, be transferred, or sell your home in less than four years, you probably should not refinance (unless you can significantly lower your costs of refinancing).

Conclusion

I recommend working with a qualified financial planner and tax advisor who can review your personal situation regarding the benefits of refinancing. They can also provide you with information on the latest tax laws.

CHAPTER 6

How to Use Home Equity Loans To Your Advantage

Wilt thou seal up the avenue of ill?
Pay every debt as if God wrote the bill!
–Ralph Waldo Emerson, *Suum Cuique*

Sleep without supping, and wake without owing.
–George Herbert, *Jacula Prudentum, No. 93*

Each year American homeowners take out millions of dollars in home equity loans. Home equity is the difference between the value of the house and what you owe on it. For example, your house today is worth $200,000 and you only owe $75,000 on your mortgage; your home's equity is $125,000. The problem, which is a major concern for many people, is that taking out a home equity loan can place you even deeper in debt. You can end up owing your lender a large sum of money that you will be unable to repay. The ultimate consequence is that you may lose your home to foreclosure. Sadly, many people take out this type of loan for the wrong reasons and end up paying this very high price. However, there are good reasons for using your home's equity. Let us now examine some of the justifiable reasons for taking equity out of your home.

Medical Emergencies

During the course of your lifetime, medical emergencies may occur. We all experience tragedies, physical set-backs, accidents, and illness. Hopefully, insurance will protect and take care of us when these emergencies occur. However, not everyone has enough insurance to cover every contingency or every unexpected event. It is sometimes necessary to quickly access more money than you have in your personal checking or savings account. In times of emergency, it may make sense to use the equity in your home.

Let us imagine that a member of your family is diagnosed with a serious illness or is involved in an automobile accident. Does your family member have adequate medical insurance? If not, it may be necessary to use some of the equity in your home so that this person can get the medical care they need.

Once the family member is healthy again and the medical bills are sufficiently paid, try to replenish your home's equity as quickly as possible for future availability.

Financial Emergencies

Just as we experience medical emergencies, we also experience financial emergencies. For example, a very common financial emergency is the loss of a job. While many people are able to find another job quickly, others go weeks, months, or even years before finding employment. Such a long period of unemployment can definitely cause a financial emergency that may necessitate withdrawing your home's equity. A few words of caution: It would be extremely difficult to obtain an equity loan if you are unemployed. You should apply for an equity line of credit while you are currently working and before any financial emergencies occur.

Another financial emergency can be the loss of money in a bad investment. For example, if your losses are substantial, you may have to use your home's equity to repay a business debt or to cover a margin call on your stock purchase(s).

Special Circumstances

Under special circumstances, a child's education would classify. Let us say your child was admitted to a university or graduate school. You might expect your child to work a certain number of hours each week to help pay for educational expenses. If there is still a shortage of money, you may want to help your child achieve his/her educational goals. If you do not have any other source of funds, it may make sense to use your home's equity to pay for this important schooling.

Some people also consider certain home improvements to fall into the special circumstances category. For example, you may be living in a relatively small home and another child may be due. Because you cannot afford or do not want to move, you decide to add another bedroom. You may want to use your home's equity if you do not have any other source of funds to pay for the room addition.

Special Investments

Over the course of your lifetime, you may come across some very special investments, opportunities or business ventures that justify borrowing against your home's equity. Before taking out a home equity loan to make such investments, you should investigate that opportunity thoroughly. Never use your home's equity to make any type of risky or speculative investments, such as buying options or commodities. If you have any other source of funds, use that money. The equity in your home should be your last choice to use for any investment. Remember, this opportunity may not work out and you may actually lose money, yet you will still have a home equity loan that must be repaid.

However, if you do decide to use your home's equity for a special investment, do not get greedy. Do not wait for your investment to triple or quadruple before you take any money out. For the purpose of safeguarding your home, you may want to take out a certain percentage or even 100% of your profits from your investment and use that money to start repaying your loan, or else you could wind up giving back some or all of your profits.

Knowing When Not to Withdraw Your Home's Equity

Just as important as knowing when to use your home's equity is knowing when you should not. You should not use your home's equity to pay for unnecessary purchases.

Perhaps the most common mistake people make is to withdraw their home's equity to make consumer purchases. You do not want to use your home's equity to buy new furniture, elaborate stereo systems, expensive art work, boats, sports cars, luxury cars, motor homes, vacation homes, or to go on expensive vacations. Certainly there is nothing wrong with buying these things, but you should make such purchases with your spendable income. Do not increase the size of your mortgage just to pay for these items. Instead, focus your attention on making more money or on saving more money to get these finer things in life.

What You Need to Understand About Home Equity Loans

There are many benefits of obtaining a home equity loan, but before you rush into getting one, consider all the ramifications. It is true that if you need cash, your home equity might be the answer since it is the cheapest credit available and, under current tax laws, the loan interest (up to $100,000 and subject to the restrictions mentioned earlier) is still tax deductible. However, the loan must be secured by your house to deduct the interest charges.

There are two basic types of equity loans. First is the **fixed-rate loan,** similar to a second mortgage. You can borrow a certain amount of money and repay it in fixed monthly payments for a specified number of years, such as, 5, 10, or 15 years. This type of loan makes sense if you need a certain amount of money now, such as for a home improvement.

The second type of equity loan is a **line of credit,** which means you have a pre-approved credit limit. This loan gives you a lot of flexibility because you can access money when you need it. You are charged interest only when you withdraw the money. For example, you might arrange for a $70,000 line of credit. If you only need $10,000 all you have to do is write a check. You will pay interest only on the $10,000 you borrowed.

Repaying the money to your line of credit is also quite flexible. The most common time period is five to ten years. For example, if the payback period is ten years, you have the option to pay both principal and interest in monthly payments, or make interest-only payments. If you make interest-only payments, at the end of ten years, you will have to pay off the loan. If you do not have the money to do this in a lump sum, then you will have to secure a new home equity loan or refinance your first mortgage.

An equity line of credit makes sense for someone who will borrow irregular amounts of money for future needs, such as a car purchase, college tuition, or just to have the money available for opportunities or emergencies. The interest rates charged on both types of loans are similar. You will pay anywhere between one and three points above the prime rate. That is far less than what you must pay for credit card debt or other unsecured loans.

Equity loans have many different options. One option is a fixed-rate loan which you can adjust if interest rates go down. Another is a line of credit that will protect an overdraft on your checking account.

The standard amount most lenders will allow you to borrow on your home's equity is 75% to 80%. Some lenders will let you borrow 100% of your equity or up to the lender's preset dollar amount. You will generally pay a few extra points for that privilege. For example, due to the preset limit, the lender will let you borrow only $100,000 even though your equity is worth $150,000. Instead of paying 7%, you will pay 9%.

There are some features you should know of when you apply for an equity loan. If you have established a line of credit, you probably will receive a checkbook, although some lenders also offer credit cards, or debit cards. Most lenders will not charge you closing costs. Many lenders will charge you $200 to $350 if you close your line of credit within one year, the exception is if you sell your house. Since you will not pay any closing costs, the lender will charge you approximately an extra ½% to 1% on the interest rate. If you decide to borrow a large amount of money it would be to your advantage to pay all the closing costs to get a lower interest rate. Many lenders will accept this arrangement. Some lenders will let you adjust rates on their equity loans. For example, if the prime rate decreases so will your equity loan, or if interest rates increase you have the option to convert your loan to a fixed-rate at whatever the prevailing rates are.

There are a few issues I want to alert you to regarding equity loans. One issue is that many people pay off their high interest and/or nondeductible interest loans with a home equity loan. They do this because the interest rate will most likely be lower and therefore the payment will be less.

Also, the interest is tax deductible. For example, you have a $20,000 automobile loan with a four-year payment plan. You decide to use $20,000 of your home's equity to pay off this auto loan. You should now repay your home equity loan with the same payment as you were making on your original auto loan. By making this same payment (the amount of the auto loan payment) you will pay off what would have been a four-year loan in less than four years. Should the situation arise when you cannot afford the payments, then you can extend the time period on your home equity loan beyond four years. By extending the time period to eight years, for example, you will have lower monthly payments—which should more comfortably fit into your budget.

When comparing home equity loans, be aware of advertisements that promote very low introductory rates—or teaser rates. Read the fine print to learn the true annual percentage rate (APR). For example, your initial interest rate might be only 7%. Your minimum monthly payment might be $400, which you can afford. However, after six months your interest rate increases and your monthly payments jump accordingly. You find you cannot afford such high payments.

Also be aware of minimum amounts that some lenders require you to borrow to get their best rates. The advertisement you see in the newspaper or the lender's front window may show an interest rate of 9%. However, the fine print states that the interest rate is only available on loans of more than $100,000. If you want to borrow only $50,000—or if you only qualify for that amount—you may end up paying 11% interest. Some lenders charge a higher interest rate for small loans and some charge a higher rate for large loans. It is definitely worth investigating what sort of breaks or reductions you might receive from your lender based on the size of the home equity loan you may be obtaining. If you apply for a jumbo loan you will pay a slightly higher interest rate. The amount considered to be a jumbo varies from lender to lender.

Check the rates with small local banks, you may be able to obtain a better rate. Also check with mortgage brokers, mortgage bankers, finance companies, and credit unions where you are a member.

Read all of your loan contracts and disclosure documents carefully. These documents will explain important information, such as the costs, fees, APR, and penalties.

Exceptions to the Tax Deduction Rules On Home Equity Loans

There are a few exceptions where you cannot deduct the interest on the equity loan. First, you may be subject to the alternative minimum tax if you are a high income earner. In this case, the interest on a home equity loan that is used for personal expenditures is not deductible for alternative minimum tax purposes. The money you borrow from your equity must be used to build, buy, or improve your first or second house to deduct the interest. Second, if you invest the money in tax-exempt bonds or a single premium life insurance policy you will not be allowed to deduct the interest. Third, if your mortgage plus the home equity loan totals more than the fair market value of the house, you cannot deduct the interest. See your tax advisor to discuss your own situation.

Conclusion

Your home is probably the largest financial investment you will ever make in your life. For many of you, it is also the best financial investment you will ever make. In addition, you get to live in your home, enjoy it, and raise a family in it while it appreciates in value. Home equity loans can enable you to use the equity in your home when and if you need it.

I recommend exercising extreme caution and restraint in using your home's equity. Utilize it only for true emergencies or in cases where you have absolutely no other source of funds. If you know for certain that you will be able to quickly and fully repay the money you draw out of your home's equity, you can be a little more liberal in withdrawing it.

CHAPTER 7

How to Make Inflation Your Ally Instead of Your Enemy

Debt is the worst poverty.

–Thomas Fuller, MD, *Gnomalogia*

He that gets out of debt grows rich.

–George Herbert, *Jacula Prudentum, No. 9*

Inflation is truly the silent thief who steals from all of us and makes many people poor—especially retirees. Inflation has rewarded those who hold hard assets (such as real estate) and has punished those who hold paper assets (such as savings accounts). It is extremely important to take inflation into account when considering the type of mortgage to apply for and also how to be in the position to pay off your mortgage as soon as possible. Let us review the following example. Say you took out a 30-year, $100,000 mortgage in 1959—that was a huge mortgage in 1959. You might have wondered, "How am I ever going to be able to pay back all this money?" What you did not consider in 1959 is how little the dollar would be worth in 20 or 30 years. For instance, you can no longer buy hamburgers for

20 cents, you cannot buy milkshakes for 10 cents. Today, the average American car now costs approximately $20,000—if you pay 8% sales tax, that comes to $1,600. In 1959, $1,600 would have bought you a new car. In 1959, your first monthly mortgage payment of $500 seemed like a fortune. In 1989, your last mortgage payment of $500 was a trivial amount.

What happened to this good economy in which almost every working person could afford to buy a home, a car, and support a family? The February 1995 issue of *Reader's Digest* contains an article on inflation titled, "You Call This a Good Economy?" The author, Jude Wanniski, makes the point that this good economy was "inflated away."

A person who could easily afford to buy a $20,000 home in 1963 cannot afford to buy a $200,000 home today. This situation is made even worse because property taxes and insurance costs have also sky-rocketed. Therefore, the person who would have been a homeowner in 1963 might today be trapped as a renter.

Why are so many people today worried about money? Inflation has seriously eroded the purchasing power of the dollar. Our after-tax incomes lose purchasing power each year. Wanniski makes the point that a minimum wage job today may pay $5 an hour, which yields $4 an hour after taxes. In the early 1950s, minimum wage jobs may have paid 75 cents per hour. Just to keep up with inflation, today's minimum wage would have to be approximately $7.50 for the same worker to be able to afford the same standard of living he/she had in the 1950s. Thus, because of inflation, millions of Americans are losing ground every year.

How Much Things Will Cost You in the Future

Item	Today	In 10 Years	In 20 Years	In 30 Years
House*	$100,000	$170,814	$291,775	$498,395
Car*	$20,000	$34,162	$58,355	$99,676
Restaurant Dinner*	$7.50	$12	$22	$37
Domestic Air Fare†	$500	$1,296	$3,363	$8,724
Gallon of Gas†	$1.35	$3.50	$9.08	$23.55

* Based on 5.5% inflation † Based on 10% inflation

As you are making your monthly mortgage payment, you will be paying back that debt with cheaper and cheaper dollars. Due to inflation, your income is likely to go up significantly over the years you have that mortgage.

Remember that inflation can make investors rich and savers poor. Look at how much money you really have by leaving your money in a savings account. If you factor in taxes and inflation, your money will lose value and purchasing power in most years that you leave it in a savings account. However, I still recommend you keep some money in the bank—you do need a savings account. History has proven that investments in quality real estate, stocks, and mutual funds have made many people wealthy. People who are savers (certificates of deposit [CD], money market accounts, bonds) have paid dearly after factoring in taxes and inflation (loss of purchasing power). I have had clients tell me they wanted a CD to guarantee their principal. What they are really saying is they do not want their principal to decrease. They want to be sure that the CD never falls below the original $10,000 investment; but, because of inflation their principal will erode. They will have $10,000 at all times, but not in purchasing power. An item that costs $10,000 in 1996, will cost more than $10,000 in the year 2000 because of inflation.

If you really want to study inflation and learn how to make it your ally rather than your enemy you must study history. History shows us that while we do sometimes have periods of low inflation or no inflation, these periods are usually very brief. Often, they are followed by periods of quite rapid inflation.

What Is the Real Rate of Inflation?

While the stated rate of inflation in recent years has averaged approximately 3%, many financial experts believe that the true rate of inflation is much higher. In fact, some financial experts are claiming the real rate of inflation is more than 10%!

Since inflation has a profound impact on all of us, it is essential to understand how the rate of inflation is arrived at. The Bureau of Labor Statistics measures inflation using the Consumer Price Index (CPI). Even many government officials admit that the CPI is not an accurate gauge of inflation.

Why do some financial experts claim the CPI is inaccurate? In the late 1970s and early 1980s, there was massive inflation in the United States. Some companies were forced to pay more than 20% for business loans and mortgage rates were in the teens.

What the government economists decided to do was to change the way that inflation was measured. In the early 1980s, government economists decided to take the costs of purchasing homes, automobiles, education, and certain other necessities of modern life out of the CPI. As a result, inflation appeared to drop. Yet, while inflation seemed to be going down, housing costs in many communities increased to more than 10% per year, and automobile and education costs increased by 10% to more than 15% per year. The news about the change in the CPI was quickly forgotten. When the CPI figures were printed, they appeared to drop and the public was placated. However, many economic experts were concerned that the CPI figures were too low and warned that true inflation was significantly higher than the government figures indicated.

Why did the government economists change the way the CPI was calculated? They decided to remove the rising costs of buying a home because not everyone has a mortgage. While it is true that not everyone has a mortgage, approximately 65% of Americans do. They decided to remove the cost of buying a new car because new models have improvements over old models and therefore are not directly comparable.

You may be wondering how much these changes lowered the official rate of inflation. During a year in which the CPI-measured rate of inflation was 4%, other studies came to the conclusion that the true rate of inflation was 12%. During a year when the CPI reported inflation to be at 5%, one of the largest accounting firms in the country remeasured it using the previous standards. They found that inflation was actually 15%. In both cases, experts found that the true rate of inflation was three times what the CPI reported it to be.

There are also a variety of other factors that make inflation seem lower than it truly is. New technologies are not included in the CPI. For example, when CD players, big screen televisions, and fax machines entered the marketplace, and even when they became commonplace, they were not included in the CPI. Tens of millions of machines using these new technologies have been purchased by consumers and yet the CPI does not reflect one cent of these hundreds of billions of dollars of expenditures.

Another major problem with the CPI is that it does not measure the quality of products sold. For example, a product made in the 1970s might have contained stainless steel whereas the 1990s version might be made with plastic. The CPI does not account for this difference. A product that previously contained all natural high-quality ingredients might be made with cheaper artificial sweeteners and extenders. The CPI does not measure this. If a stainless steel product from a few years ago was compared with a stainless steel product today (rather than a plastic product), we might see that the real rate of inflation over that time period was 40%.

Other Powerful Factors Affecting Inflation

There are numerous other powerful factors at work in our society that are contributing to inflation but are not measured by the antiquated CPI. More than one million Americans are now infected with human immunodeficiency virus (HIV) and may develop and die from acquired immunodeficiency syndrome (AIDS) at a cost of billions of dollars to the healthcare industry. The CPI does not account for this. Huge national disasters like the California earthquakes, the floods in the midwest and south, and hurricanes are not accounted for in inflation figures. Add to this the billions that will have to be spent on our crumbling highways, subways, dams, and bridges. Is any of this accounted for in the CPI figures? No.

You may ask what relevance all of this has to you. Let us assume inflation stays at a modest 4% per year. If you retire on an income of $30,000 a year, in 10 years you will need $44,000 a year just to maintain your same lifestyle, and in 25 years you will need $80,000. You could be in very serious financial trouble because most pensions do not have cost of living increases. For many people, the only alternative is to withdraw money from their savings and use the principal for living expenses.

The good news about inflation is that you will be paying off your home mortgage with dollars that are worth less and less. For this reason, if no other, it is wise to keep your mortgage as long as possible. Plus, you will receive valuable tax deductions and appreciation on your house. Whatever extra money you have should be invested outside your mortgage where it may grow faster than inflation.

Just how much less could a dollar be worth? Let us look at a ten-year time period and assume your mortgage payment is $1,000 a month. If inflation is only 3% a year, in ten years your $1,000 mortgage payment would really only represent $744 in buying power. Another way of looking at this is to say that you are paying today's $1,000 debt with only $744 in future money.

If inflation averages 5%, in ten years you will be paying your $1,000 mortgage with only $614 of real money. If inflation averages 6%, you will only have to pay $558 a month in real money because the value of the dollar will have declined so much. If inflation averages 10%, you will only be paying $386 per month in real money on your $1,000 monthly mortgage payment. Plus, you will probably be earning much more money and you will be taking home many more dollars each month because of inflation. Do you now clearly see how valuable it is to delay paying off your mortgage as long as you can, so that you can pay it off with cheaper dollars?

Let us now review how inflation and taxes can affect your mortgage. If you have an 8% mortgage and you are in the 36% tax bracket, your net cost is only a little over 5% after you factor in your tax deduction. If inflation is 3%, your real net cost of your mortgage is only 2%.

How Inflation Can Make a Millionaire Not Live Like a Millionaire

The dream of many Americans is to become a millionaire. A big surprise awaits those who think they will be rich if they can just accumulate $1,000,000. Let us say you were able to get 7% interest on your $1,000,000 to yield an annual income of $70,000. Could you improve your standard of living? Probably not. Especially not after you paid 33% in taxes, which would reduce your net income to only $46,900. The $46,900 is further reduced due to the effects of inflation.

Most people do not want to touch their principal. However, if they do use part of their principal, their future earnings—interest—will be reduced because they are earning interest on less principal. So, they have to once again use part of their principal, which will result in earning less money. This vicious cycle can quickly deplete most or all of their savings. People become very stressful when they have to use part of the principal from their savings and investments. But inflation may force them to spend part of their principal to financially make ends meet. Furthermore, to counteract the effects of inflation you must actually add to your principal. If you do not add to your principal you will lose purchasing power each year and your standard of living will steadily decline. It is important to make some investments in promising stocks, mutual funds, and other real estate that can possibly keep pace with inflation or outperform it.

To cope with inflation and the higher cost of living, unions, professionals, government workers, school teachers, police, retirees and millions of other people each year demand cost-of-living increases, which creates still more inflation. This is the reality of inflation and how it robs all of us—even millionaires—of our purchasing power.

Inflation and the Tax Consequences Of Selling a House and Buying a New One

When a home is sold and a new one purchased, there can be significant tax benefits. These tax benefits will depend on the price of the new house purchased and the old one sold.

For example, a married couple purchased their house for $200,000 and then sold it for $300,000. Due to inflation, the house appreciated in value and their profit was $100,000. The purchase price of their new home is $400,000. Since the new house costs more than the prior home, there will not be any taxes owed on the sale if the new house is built or purchased within two years before or after the old home is sold. Be aware of the fact that the gain will reduce the tax basis on the new house.

What if they bought a new house that cost less than what they sold the previous home for? Using our above example, the new house costs $250,000. They would have to pay capital gains tax on $50,000 because the cost of the new house is less than the amount realized on the sale of the prior residence ($300,000). However, if they were to make $50,000 worth of improvements in the new home before two years expire, they could defer the capital gains tax.

Finally, you should also know that the law would allow this couple to exclude from their income the first $125,000 gain realized on the sale of their principal residence. However, this couple must meet three requirements: 1) one of them must be at least 55 years old on the date of the sale, 2) they must file a joint tax return, and 3) the spouse who is 55 or older must own the home and live in it as his/her principal residence for at least three out of five years prior to the sale. These three years need not be consecutive. This exclusion is only available once per lifetime, regardless of how much of the exclusion is actually used.

All homeowners, including single, divorced, or widowed, should see their tax advisor to discuss their personal situation.

Conclusion

To make inflation your ally, you should have a 30-year mortgage. By having a 30-year mortgage you will have the lowest monthly payments. You will then be taking advantage of inflation by paying off your mortgage with cheaper and cheaper dollars each year. Inflation will further benefit you because your home will appreciate in value. In addition, a 30-year mortgage will provide you with the maximum tax deductions.

CHAPTER

8

The Mortgage Controversy: 15-Year Versus 30-Year Mortgages

Words pay no debts.

–William Shakespeare, *Troilus and Cressida*

Dreading that climax of all human ills,
the inflammation of his weekly bills.

–Lord Byron, *Don Juan*

Fifteen-year mortgages have become quite popular. Perhaps you may have one. Some lenders are now even offering ten-year mortgages.

Like many people, you may think you know all there is to know about 15-year and 30-year conventional mortgages. Some of the traditional thinking about 15-year mortgages is that they are somehow better than 30-year mortgages. There have been newspaper and magazine articles trying to prove the superiority of 15-year mortgages. However, as you will discover, there are times when traditional thinking will not serve your best interests.

To compare the advantages and disadvantages of 15-year and 30-year mortgages, review the following example of one couple as they search for a home mortgage. Jim and Karen found the ideal house. It costs $120,000, and since they are putting $20,000 down, they need to find a $100,000 mortgage. They have learned the general guideline is to figure 28% of your gross monthly income should be used to pay the total mortgage payments, which include principal, interest, real estate taxes, and insurance. The 28% rate may vary and depends on other factors, such as your current outstanding monthly debts.

Jim and Karen are in their early thirties and plan to work for another 30 to 35 years before retiring. Traditionally, most young couples in their position would have gone for a 30-year conventional home mortgage. However, several of Jim and Karen's friends are pleased with the 15-year mortgages they obtained, and now Jim and Karen are wondering if they should get a 15-year mortgage, too.

While they are optimistic about their earning power, Jim and Karen are concerned about having a mortgage for 30 years. They begin to think that a 15-year mortgage is a better idea. After all, they would pay their house off quicker and then they could use that mortgage money for other things.

Jim and Karen begin their research. They go to the library and read articles about 15-year and 30-year mortgages. They talk with bankers, mortgage brokers, and financial planners. They get lots of conflicting advice, which leaves them even more confused. From the information they receive, they list the following advantages and disadvantages of 15-year and 30-year conventional mortgages.

15-Year Mortgage

Advantages

- Mortgage paid in 15 years
- Less total interest paid (can be more than 50% less)
- Lower interest rate possible
- Quicker build-up of equity

Disadvantages

- Larger monthly payments are required
- Requires more income to qualify for this mortgage
- Ties up greater percentage of your income each month

30-Year Mortgage

Advantages

- Lower monthly payments
- Easier qualification for a mortgage because less income is required to qualify

Disadvantages

- It takes 30 years to pay off the mortgage
- More total interest will be paid
- Slower equity build-up

Jim and Karen decide to get the 15-year mortgage at 8½%. They chose a 15-year mortgage because they wanted to build up equity faster than could be accomplished with a 30-year mortgage. They wanted this equity build up in case they decided to take out a home equity loan or a larger mortgage sometime in the future.

The monthly payments are 22% higher on a 15-year mortgage compared with a 30-year mortgage. (The 15-year mortgage payments are $985* versus $769 for the 30-year. Note that the mortgage payments on a 15-year mortgage are not twice as large as a 30-year mortgage.) However, their total interest payments during the length of the mortgage

*All numbers have been rounded.

will be approximately 44% less with a 15-year mortgage as compared with the 30-year mortgage. Each year the percentage of their monthly payment going toward the principal goes up and the percentage applied toward the interest goes down. With a 15-year mortgage they are paying less in interest and thus, their tax savings are reduced. Even though the higher monthly payments will lower their monthly spendable income, they believe it is worthwhile not to have to pay all that interest.

An Analysis of Jim and Karen's 15-Year Mortgage

Jim and Karen believed they were lucky to get the 15-year mortgage. They were both working and the combination of their incomes qualified them for this mortgage and its higher monthly payments.

After a few years, Jim and Karen wanted to have children. However, when the couple looked at their finances and the high monthly mortgage payment they were locked into, it did not seem possible that they could afford to have children. Karen believed that a mother should stay at home with her children for at least a couple of years. Since interest rates were high, it did not make sense to refinance. Jim and Karen realistically accepted the fact that they could not get by and make their big monthly mortgage payments with the 15-year mortgage on Jim's salary alone. Therefore, they reluctantly decided to put off having a family.

As the years went by, Jim and Karen proudly noticed they were really paying down their mortgage principal. However, they were not very happy when it came time to complete their tax returns. They found their mortgage deduction was rapidly shrinking. By this time, their 15-year mortgage had amortized so much that they were making almost all principal payments and very little went to interest. They were paying income taxes at nearly the maximum rate.

Unexpectedly, Jim was laid off from work. They still had large mortgage payments and very little money in savings. What savings they had were quickly used up when Jim could not find a job. The couple realized they could no longer afford to make those large monthly mortgage payments. Since Jim was unemployed, the couple could not apply for a new mortgage with lower monthly payments. As a result they put their house up for sale. Unfortunately, there were many homes for sale in their neighborhood. Jim and Karen had to lower the price on their home. They accepted less money than they should have just to sell the house and get out of the mortgage.

Fifteen-year mortgages are great for some people. However, the 15-year mortgage was not a good choice for Jim and Karen. Looking back, Jim and Karen now wish they had taken out a 30-year mortgage with the lower monthly payments and higher tax deductions.

Invest Your Tax Savings

Let us look at another situation involving Jim and Karen. In this example, we will assume Jim and Karen did not have any financial difficulties. They had a $100,000, 15-year mortgage at 8½% and were in the 31% tax bracket. Their monthly payments were $985. In the 31% tax bracket, the value of their first year tax deduction was $2,594. Assume they will retire in 30 years. What if they had invested their tax savings for the remaining 29 years before retirement? What would it be worth? The value of their second year tax deduction was $2,499. What if they had invested that for the next 28 years until they retired?

When you give your money to the government in the form of taxes you no longer have it to invest, which is a guaranteed 100% loss. When you save that money from a legitimate tax deduction, such as mortgage interest, you do have that money to invest, which can grow year after year. You avoid the lost future earnings* cost, which will be discussed in Chapter 9.

Let us assume Jim and Karen invested their tax savings from the mortgage interest deduction for all 15 years of the mortgage at an 8½% return. Then, they continued to let that money grow for the next 15 years until they retired. What would those tax savings be worth? They would have $199,082—which they could use for retirement. This example shows the power of investing your tax savings year after year. You do not have to be an investment expert to accomplish this. Since 1929, the stock market has averaged more than 9%. If Jim and Karen had invested in the stock market and earned 9%, they would have had more than $225,000 when they retired.

If Jim and Karen had a larger mortgage with even more tax savings, they would have had that much more to invest. They might easily have been able to accumulate $500,000 or more by investing their tax savings.

As exciting as this example is for the 15-year mortgage, it gets even better for the 30-year mortgage. If Jim and Karen had taken out a 30-year, $100,000 mortgage at 8½%, their tax savings in the 31% bracket would be $2,626 the first year. At the end of 12 years the tax savings would still be $2,265. However, with the 15-year mortgage their tax savings in the twelfth year would only be $949. As you can see, with a 30-year mortgage, there are more tax savings available to invest. Why not invest them where they can grow every year?

With the 15-year mortgage, if the tax deductions were invested, Jim and Karen would have accumulated only $199,082. If they had a 30-year mortgage and invested all of their tax savings each year for 30 years, they would have accumulated more than $308,000, which would be an additional $108,000.

---

* *Lost future earnings* and *loss of future earnings* are interchangeable. In this book, we will use lost future earnings.

Can you see the power of this principle? As exciting as this is for a $100,000 mortgage, it is even more dramatic and more powerful for a $200,000 or $400,000 mortgage. If you take out a larger, 30-year mortgage, and invest those tax savings, the amount you will accumulate will be substantial.

You might have thought you knew everything there was to know about comparing 15-year and 30-year mortgages. However, you may not have fully understood or known how to use the powerful principle of the lost future earnings cost and investing the tax savings.

Earlier you read about the problems that Jim and Karen encountered with their 15-year mortgage. I would now like to share with you a case that will illustrate new points about a 30-year mortgage that we have not yet covered.

A 30-Year Mortgage Success Story

Robert rented a one-bedroom apartment in Chicago's Lincoln Park, a trendy neighborhood close to Lake Michigan and just north of downtown Chicago. He enjoyed the park, lake, and proximity to a variety of social activities. The only thing he did not enjoy was the fact that he was paying rent and at the end of the year had nothing to show for it. Robert wanted his own home.

Robert was disciplined and saved enough money for a down payment on a two-bedroom condominium. He bought the condo and found that he was saving more than $3,000 a year on his taxes due to the mortgage interest deduction on his 30-year mortgage.

He made several friends in his building, one of whom was Tricia. Tricia also owned a condo but wanted to live in a house someday.

Robert and Tricia married two years later. They decided to sell their condos and look for a house to buy. They were shocked at how much their condos had appreciated in value.

Robert sold his condo and made a profit of $139,000. Tricia did even better. She had a two-bedroom unit higher up in the building with a great view. Her profit was $152,000.

When Robert combined his $139,000 with Tricia's $152,000 they had $291,000 to use toward a new home. They ended up buying a beautiful five-bedroom house for $647,000. They took out a 30-year mortgage and were able to use their mortgage interest deduction to reduce their income taxes.

Robert and Tricia made an interesting discovery. A 30-year mortgage gave them much more financial flexibility than a 15-year mortgage. The couple learned that they could voluntarily pay down their mortgage any time they wanted. They could always make the same payments on their 30-year mortgage that a 15-year mortgage would require. They could reduce as much principal as they wanted each month. In other words, they had the ability to treat their 30-year mortgage like a 15-year mortgage if they wanted. For example, let us say your 15-year monthly mortgage payment is $1,000. You decide you want a 30-year mortgage to receive the higher tax deductions. Your payments would be $700 a month. Later on, you decide you want to use the strategy of prepayments to pay off your mortgage. You still have the option to pay $1,000 a month to your lender. The extra $300 goes toward the principal. If you have a problem one month and cannot pay $1,000, you only need to pay $700. Therefore, you are not forced to make the higher monthly payments that the 15-year mortgage requires. Almost everyone who has a 30-year mortgage can do this.

Robert and Tricia decided to pay down their 30-year mortgage as if it were a 10-year mortgage. What about the loss of their tax deduction from the declining mortgage interest write-off? They did not worry about it because they bought an apartment building that provided large mortgage interest deductions. They were also able to depreciate the building to further reduce their income taxes. You cannot do that with your own personal home.

Today, Robert and Tricia only owe $83,000 on their beautiful house, which was recently appraised at nearly $855,000.

A New Look at the 15-Year Versus 30-Year Mortgage Controversy

Let us build on the original comparison done by Jim and Karen of the advantages and disadvantages of 15-year and 30-year mortgages.

15-Year Mortgage

Advantages

- Mortgage paid in 15 years
- Less total interest paid (can be more than 50% less)
- Lower interest rate possible
- Quicker buildup of equity
- Equity may be available through home equity loans to pay off nondeductible consumer interest debts.
- Forced savings—equity (important if home owner is a "spender")
- College financial aid might become more available. The standard financial aid forms do not count home equity as a parental asset.
- Quicker ownership that may also have psychological benefits

Disadvantages

- Larger monthly payments are required.
- Lower tax deductions as interest portion of monthly payment rapidly decreases
- Less tax savings means less money to spend or invest.

- Ties up greater percentage of your income each month, due to the higher monthly payments
- Reduces funds available for savings/investment (where they could earn a higher return than the interest you are paying on the mortgage)
- Higher lost future earnings cost
- Requires more income to qualify
- Temptation to take out a loan against the growing equity for luxury spending (for example, vacations, cars)
- Could be vulnerable to litigation due to increased equity

30-Year Mortgage

Advantages

- Larger tax deductions: As your income increases, this safe tax deduction becomes even more valuable.
- Lower monthly payments
- You can invest the difference in payments between the 30-year and 15-year mortgage.
- You can invest the additional tax savings from your increased tax deduction.
- Financial and budgeting flexibility: Whenever it is convenient, you can prepay the mortgage principal; you are not locked into high mortgage payments.
- Easier qualification for a mortgage because less income is required to qualify
- Could protect your home against possible litigation. Equity build-up is slower, making it less attractive to potential litigants.

Disadvantages

- It takes 30 years to pay off.
- More interest paid
- Slower equity buildup
- Longer period during which your mortgage is subject to government regulations (for example, government could reduce or eliminate mortgage interest deduction)

Comparing the First 15 Years Of a 30-Year Mortgage with a 15-Year Mortgage

You should look at a 30-year mortgage for only the first 15 years and compare it at the end of this time frame with a 15-year mortgage. The first big difference, of course, is that the 15-year mortgage is paid off.

The second difference is that you obviously have paid more into a 15-year mortgage than you would have paid in the first 15 years of a 30-year mortgage. The difference in monthly mortgage payments is available to invest each month. With a 30-year mortgage, the majority of your payments the first 15 years are applied to interest, which is tax deductible. In addition, you would receive much larger tax deductions from the first 15 years of a 30-year mortgage than you would from the entire 15-year mortgage. How much greater is the tax break offered by the 30-year mortgage if we compare identical 15-year time periods?

On a $100,000, 15-year mortgage at 8½%, you would receive a total of $23,948 in tax savings over the term of the mortgage. This assumes you are in the 31% tax bracket. If you had a 30-year mortgage for the same amount, at the same interest rate, and the same 31% tax bracket, during those same 15 years, you would have had $36,111 in tax savings—even though your monthly payments were 22% lower with the 30-year mortgage. (The monthly mortgage payment for the 15-year mortgage is $985; the 30-year mortgage payment is $769.)

If you had a $200,000, 15-year mortgage at the same 8½% interest rate, and the same 31% tax bracket, you would receive $47,897 in tax savings. Compare this with a 30-year mortgage for the same $200,000 with the same interest rate and the same tax bracket. During those same 15 years, you would have had $72,222 in tax savings. Your tax savings is an additional $24,325 on a 30-year mortgage.

If you had a $500,000, 15-year mortgage at the same interest rate and tax bracket, you would receive a tax savings of $119,742 during the term of this mortgage. For a 30-year mortgage with the same $500,000 amount, same interest rate and tax bracket, during those same 15 years you would have saved $180,555 in taxes. This is in addition to the fact that your monthly mortgage payments were less with the 30-year mortgage. This difference in monthly mortgage payments, as well as the tax savings, can be invested.

It really gets fascinating when you compare the total value of the tax deductions for 15-year and 30-year mortgages over their full terms. A $100,000, 15-year mortgage at 8½% gives you a total tax savings of $23,948 if you are in the 31% tax bracket. If you have a 30-year mortgage, you would get $54,811 in tax savings for borrowing this same amount of money at the same interest rate. Your tax savings are more than 100% greater with the 30-year mortgage, plus you can invest all those tax savings and make them grow tremendously over 30 years.

A $200,000, 15-year mortgage at 8½% gives you a total tax savings of $47,897 over the term of the mortgage if you are in the 31% tax bracket. If you had a 30-year mortgage for the same amount, and if you were in the same tax bracket, you would receive a total tax savings of $109,621 (again, over twice as much). Of course, you would also be able to invest those tax savings each year.

A $500,000, 15-year mortgage at 8½% interest gives you a total tax savings of $119,742. A 30-year mortgage for the identical amount and with the identical interest rate would give you a substantial $274,053 in tax savings. It should now be obvious that a 30-year mortgage does have far greater tax savings than a 15-year mortgage. Remember, with a 15-year mortgage your tax savings end in 15 years. With a 30-year mortgage, they continue for its full term.

Why not take full advantage of your tax deductions? Let us say that you buy a $150,000 home and finance the purchase with a 30-year mortgage. Why not invest your tax savings every year? Most people have little or nothing to show for their tax deductions after their home is paid off. Depending on your investment returns, the amount of your tax savings, and how many years you discipline yourself to make these investments, you will accumulate a large sum of money for your retirement. You can also use this money to pay cash for a second home. This second home can be used for pleasure or as an investment. If you decide to use your house as an investment, you can collect rent from it and use the money to supplement your other retirement income.

Here is another very interesting scenario. Let us refer to our example of a $100,000 mortgage at 8½% and a 31% tax bracket. A 15-year mortgage would have monthly payments of $985 and a 30-year mortgage $769. The difference is $216. One choice is to take out a 15-year mortgage and pay your monthly mortgage payments for 15 years and then invest the same $985 a month for the next 15 years toward retirement. Your other choice would be to take out a 30-year mortgage and pay the monthly payments of $769 for 30 years. You can invest the difference of $216 every month for the next 30 years. Which option would produce more money? The results will surprise you. They are identical. Both choices of investing give you the same $356,000 when invested at 8½%. However the 30-year mortgage makes more sense because you will receive much larger tax deductions.

By now, you may be convinced that 30-year mortgages do have many important advantages over 15-year mortgages. With a 30-year mortgage you will pay more interest charges than with a 15-year mortgage, but that will only apply if you pay the 30-year mortgage for its full term. Keep in mind you have the option to pay off your 30-year mortgage in 15 years or less. I do not mean to imply that you should never consider a 15-year mortgage. They may be beneficial for some people.

A 15-Year Mortgage Success Story

Charles is a 55-year-old physician with an established practice in internal medicine. Charles' second wife, Alice, teaches at a local elementary school. They got married last year.

Recently they bought a home in one of Chicago's suburbs. While Charles and Alice are at a comfortable stage in their lives, they are concerned about their retirement.

Charles and Alice now want to make absolutely certain they are able to retire in approximately 15 years. For this reason, they obtained a 15-year mortgage on their recent home purchase. Charles likes the forced savings aspect of his mortgage because it builds equity. He knows that if he has to send the money to the lender each month he will not be able to spend it elsewhere.

Charles and Alice are excited about the possibility of retiring mortgage free. They are willing to give up much of their mortgage interest tax deduction to make absolutely sure that their home is indeed paid off in 15 years. A number of years ago, Charles lost a great deal of money in risky investments. "At this point in my life," he says, "I don't have the time or interest to worry about where to invest my money. I just want to enjoy life. I'd rather invest my money in my house."

Charles and Alice will retire mortgage free in 15 years if they follow their plan. If real estate prices continue to appreciate in their neighborhood the way they have in the past, their $300,000 home will be worth more than $500,000 in 15 years. For Charles and Alice, the psychological benefits, such as peace of mind, and financial security of being able to retire mortgage free in 15 years, outweigh the higher tax deductions and the lower monthly mortgage payments that a 30-year mortgage would have provided.

The Final Analysis: 15-Year Versus 30-Year Mortgages

Why do most people take out a 15-year mortgage instead of a 30-year mortgage? Two main reasons: (1) they want to pay off their mortgage in 15 years, not 30 years; and/or (2) they want to save money because they will pay less interest to the lender on a 15-year mortgage. The 15-year mortgage is not nearly as financially sensible as it appears to be. Why not take out a 30-year mortgage, get larger tax deductions, have lower monthly mortgage payments, and pay off your mortgage in ten years or less. Furthermore, if you do pay off your 30-year mortgage in ten years or less, you will save a substantial amount of interest. You may be able to save even more interest than with a 15-year mortgage.

Another important advantage that the 30-year mortgage has over the 15-year mortgage is that you have the opportunity to invest the difference in monthly mortgage payments. You should be able to earn a higher return on your investments than what the mortgage interest is costing you. If interest rates decline, you have the option to refinance to a lower interest rate. Thus, you can invest the difference in monthly mortgage payments where they will have the possibility of earning an even higher rate of return.

Finally, there is one more important advantage of a 30-year mortgage. Millions of people contribute money to a 401(k) retirement plan or individual retirement account (IRA). One of the primary reasons to have a 401(k) or IRA is to receive current tax savings. By combining a 30-year mortgage and a 401(k) or IRA, you will achieve the maximum overall tax savings each year. Let us use an example. You have a tax-deductible IRA to which you contribute $2,000. If your tax bracket is 30%, your current tax savings are $600 ($2,000 x 30%.) Let us assume you have a 30-year mortgage and your current tax savings are $3,000. With a 15-year mortgage the current tax savings would be only $2,200. When you combine your IRA with a 15-year mortgage, the current total tax savings are only $2,800. When combined with your 30-year mortgage, your current total tax savings are $3,600. As you can see, your 30-year mortgage provides $800 in additional tax savings. That is smart tax planning. With a 15-year mortgage the tax savings are $800 less. This $800 loss is more than the current tax savings of $600 from your IRA. This is poor tax planning. It is important to note that 401(k)s and IRAs are only tax-deferral programs. Mortgage interest deductions are true tax deductions.

The Question of the 40-Year Mortgage

If 30-year mortgages are so great, are 40-year mortgages even better? Usually not. As you may recall, there is quite a difference between the payments on a 15-year mortgage and a 30-year mortgage. A $100,000, 30-year mortgage at 8% will have a monthly payment of $734. A 40-year mortgage will have a monthly payment of $695, just $39 less than the 30-year mortgage. However, on a 40-year mortgage you will have mortgage payments for an extra ten years. Using our example, after 30 years you would still owe $57,309 in principal and $26,129 in interest. After 40 years, you would have paid $233,750 in interest compared with $164,155 on a 30-year mortgage. If you are in a 28% tax bracket, after 40 years the tax savings would be $65,450. On the 30-year mortgage, you would have saved $45,963 in taxes.

As you have just seen, a 40-year mortgage saves you very little money each month and it builds up very little equity. For those two reasons alone, I do not recommend the 40-year mortgage. It is important that you build up some equity in your mortgage, if for no other reason than the fact that real estate prices do fluctuate.

Are 40-year mortgages suitable for anyone? Yes. If you are a successful and disciplined investor you may wish to consider a 40-year mortgage. Using our example, you can invest the additional $39 every month. For example, I know someone who consistently earns between 15% and 25% per year investing in his business. It would be foolish for him to tie up money in his home. If you can earn high returns in the stock market, or from some other form of investing, you may wish to consider getting a 40-year mortgage so that you would have the maximum amount of money available each month for investing.

CHAPTER 9

The Lost Future Earnings Cost

A creditor is worse than a master; for a master owns only your person, a creditor owns your dignity and can belabor that.

–Victor Hugo, *Les Miserables*

First payments is what made us think we were prosperous, and the other nineteen is what showed us we were broke.

–Will Rogers, *Autobiography*

One of the greatest financial losses most people experience in their lives is the *lost future earnings** cost. I sometimes refer to this as "lost opportunity cost." It is also called the "cost of not investing," or Lost Investment of Future Earnings ("LIFE of your money"). After reading this chapter you will understand why the lost future earnings cost will amount to a substantial amount of money.

This lost future earnings cost is not known and/or not understood by many financial planners and other financial advisors. The general public has even less awareness of this

* *Lost future earnings* and *loss of future earnings* are interchangeable. In this book I will use lost future earnings.

important money principle. The best way for me to explain it is to use examples. Picture in your mind: You have a wealthy relative who will let you live in his/her furnished house for the next 30 years. Your relative will put in writing that you do not have to make any mortgage payments for the next 30 years. Your only obligation is that you must invest the same amount of money every month that you would otherwise have been required to pay a lender in monthly mortgage payments. After 30 years, whatever amount of money you have accumulated can be used for your retirement. The house will be paid in full and you will then become the new owner. Let us say that if you had to make mortgage payments, they would have been $1,000 a month (principal and interest). You invested that money every month for 30 years at 8%. You have accumulated more than $1,400,000 (pre-tax).

Unfortunately, most of us are not lucky enough to find ourselves in this position. Since you do have to make mortgage payments and cannot invest $1,000 a month, you will give up more than $1,400,000 in future earnings. This is a real loss of money. The purpose of explaining the lost future earnings cost is to teach you the real cost of your home. It is important to remember that money has future value if it is invested. If money is spent it has a lost future earnings cost. A major mistake most people make when determining the total cost of their house is to multiply $1,000 per month (principal and interest) by 360 months (30-year mortgage), which comes to a total of $360,000. The real cost as you have seen is more than $1,400,000, not $360,000.

Let us further explore the lost future earnings cost from our example. Since your wealthy relative will allow you to live in his/her house, you now have available $20,000 to invest which otherwise would have been your down payment. If you invested $20,000 at 8% for 30 years, your money would accumulate to more than $200,000 (pre-tax). If you had to use the $20,000 for a down payment instead of investing it, your lost future earnings cost would have been $200,000. As you can clearly see, your total lost future earnings cost from your mortgage payments of $1,000 a month and your $20,000 down payment is more than $1,600,000 ($200,000 + $1,400,000). Let us say, after 30 years your home has appreciated to $500,000. If you subtract the $500,000 from your lost future earnings cost of $1,600,000 you still have a substantial cost (loss) on your home. Unfortunately, this critical money principle—lost future earnings cost—is neither considered nor understood when you purchase a home or obtain a mortgage. We have not even considered the lost future earnings cost on real estate taxes, insurance or home improvements.

Now let us look at how the lost future earnings cost will reduce the profit from the sale of your home. We will assume you originally paid $100,000 for your house. Fifteen years later you decide to sell it for $150,000, which you believe is a $50,000 profit. We will now review why it is misleading to think you made a $50,000 profit. We will assume you paid $20,000 down payment on the original purchase price. Your $20,000 has a lost future earnings cost because you did not earn any money on your down payment. If you had the opportunity to invest that $20,000 at 8% it would be worth $66,138 in 15 years. When you sold your house, you received back your original $20,000 down payment without interest. Your lost future earnings cost is $46,138 ($66,138–$20,000). Your house appreciated $50,000 (profit), but you forfeited $46,138 of earnings on your $20,000 down payment. As you can see, the $50,000 profit begins to vanish quickly. Remember, you will always have a lost future earnings cost on your down payment as long as you own your home. You must consider the lost future earnings cost on your down payment to arrive at an accurate profit when you sell your home. However, the IRS does not consider the lost future earnings cost when calculating your $50,000 profit for tax purposes.

Many homeowners have been advised to make their down payment as large as possible to reduce their monthly mortgage payments. If you make a smaller down payment, you will have control of your money and also the opportunity to earn interest on your money, plus the benefits of the increased tax deductions. By avoiding a large down payment, you will not be paying more income taxes than necessary.

Does the lost future earnings principle only apply to mortgages? The answer is no. What if your employer offered you a company car to drive at no expense? You probably would be really excited because you were going to buy a new car anyway. Instead of paying $20,000 cash for that new car you decide to invest the money in a mutual fund and believe you can average 9% a year. Let us find out how much money you would have in 10 years, 20 years, and 30 years:

$20,000 invested at 9%	for 10 years	**$ 49,000***
	for 20 years	**$120,000**
	for 30 years	**$294,000**

The point here is, if you had to purchase a $20,000 car, you would have a lost opportunity cost of $294,000 in 30 years. By having the opportunity to invest the money in a mutual fund, you would have accumulated $294,000. This is an opportunity gain. Remember, if you had purchased a car, the lost future earnings cost would not have stopped after just 30 years. It would have been lost forever! The lost future earnings cost applies to all money situations.

* All numbers have been rounded.

Paying Cash for a House Versus A 15-Year and a 30-Year Mortgage

Now let us say that you are purchasing a home for $150,000. After examining your financial options, you realize that you can either pay cash for the house or take out a mortgage.

Most homeowners who pay cash for their house think they are saving money by not paying interest to the lender. In reality, they are not saving any money at all. Let us use our previous example of your wealthy relative. Instead of paying $150,000 cash for your new home, you are now able to invest the money. By investing $150,000 at 8%, in 30 years you will have accumulated $1,509,000 (pre-tax). Had you paid cash for the house your lost future earnings cost would have been $1,509,000. If you are like most people, you will probably be shocked at the substantial amount of money you will lose because of the lost future earnings cost.

I will now compare paying cash for your home versus a 15-year and 30-year mortgage. Let us assume the house costs $250,000. Your down payment is 20%, which is $50,000. The mortgage is for $200,000 at 8% interest. Your tax bracket is 28%. Your alternative investments can also earn 8%. I will calculate the lost future earnings cost for a period of 30 years. Remember, your $50,000 down payment also has a lost future earnings cost.

Paying Cash

Gross Lost Future Earnings Cost	**$2,733,935**
Less: Value of Tax Savings Invested	**$ 0**
Net Lost Future Earnings Cost	**$2,733,935**

15-Year Mortgage

Gross Lost Future Earnings Cost	**$2,733,935**
Less: Value of Tax Savings Invested	**$ 369,944**
Net Lost Future Earnings Cost	**$2,363,991**

30-Year Mortgage

Gross Lost Future Earnings Cost	**$2,733,935**
Less: Value of Tax Savings Invested	**$ 581,818**
Net Lost Future Earnings Cost	**$2,152,117**

As these examples prove, paying cash, a 15-year mortgage, or a 30-year mortgage all have identical gross lost future earnings costs. The only difference is the tax deductions. A 30-year mortgage will provide the largest. When you pay cash for a house you have no tax deductions. Therefore, when you factor in these valuable deductions, a 30-year mortgage costs less than either paying cash for a house or a 15-year mortgage. This is one important reason why a 30-year mortgage makes the most financial sense for the majority of homeowners.

There is still another important reason to have a 30-year mortgage. You can generally invest your money in alternative investments which will earn a higher rate of return than the relatively low cost of your mortgage. For example, if you have an 8% mortgage, your true cost of money is only 5.36% (33% tax bracket). If you are in a lower tax bracket, your cost of money is higher than 5.36% because your tax deductions are less. If you are in a higher tax bracket, your cost of money is lower. (See your tax advisor regarding the phase-out rules for exemptions and itemized deductions for high income earners.) Using 5.36% as a base figure, you must ask yourself this question: Can I invest the money somewhere else and earn more than 5.36% on an after-tax basis? If the answer is "no," paying cash would make more sense. If the answer is "yes," then you should have a mortgage. It should not be difficult to earn more than 5.36%. In the past, quality stocks and mutual funds have averaged more than 9% per year.

Now, let us continue to compare paying cash for a house versus a 15-year mortgage and a 30-year mortgage. Let us assume your house cost $150,000 and you made a down payment of $30,000. If you had $150,000 cash and only put $30,000 down on your home, you would have $120,000 to invest in alternative investments that could yield more than 5.36% a year. At 10% return per year, the $120,000 would produce $12,000 in extra income. Your investments would earn almost twice as much (on a pre-tax basis) as your mortgage would cost you (5.36%).

A More In-Depth Look At the Lost Future Earnings Cost

Let us now explore the lost future earnings cost on a mortgage year by year. For example, you have a $100,000, 30-year mortgage at 8%. Your tax bracket is 28%. Your monthly mortgage payment is $734. At the end of the first year, you would have paid $835 toward the principal and $7,970 in interest. Since the interest is fully tax deductible, your tax savings on the interest would be $2,232. Deducting your tax savings of $2,232 from the gross interest you paid leaves you with a net interest cost of $5,738. Adding back in the portion of principal you are repaying ($835) you would have a net cost of $6,573.

Gross Interest	**$7,970**
Less: Tax Savings	**$2,232**
Net Interest Cost	**$5,738**
Add: Principal Repayment	**$ 835**
Total Net Cost for Year 1	**$6,573**

This is your total actual out-of-pocket expense for the first year of your mortgage (principal and interest only). If you could have invested that $6,573 at 8% for 30 years, you would have accumulated more than $71,000. Therefore, the real cost of your home for the first year is $71,000, which is the lost future earnings cost of your money. There is quite a difference between $6,573 and $71,000. Another way to make this point clear is after 30 years you will not have available the $71,000. Every dollar you have can either be used for expenses or investments (expenses = lost future earnings cost; investments = opportunity gain.)

Let us review Year 2 of this mortgage:

Gross Interest	**$7,900**
Less: Tax Savings	**$2,212**
Net Interest Cost	**$5,688**
Add: Principal Repayment	**$ 905**
Total Net Cost for Year 2	**$6,593**

If you could invest the $6,593 at 8% for 29 years, you would have accumulated more than $66,000. As you again can see, your lost future earnings, which is your real cost, is $66,000. There is a big difference between $6,593 and $66,000.

Finally, let us review Year 3 of this mortgage:

Gross Interest	**$7,825**
Less: Tax Savings	**$2,191**
Net Interest Cost	**$5,634**
Add: Principal Repayment	**$ 980**
Total Net Cost for Year 3	**$6,614**

If you had the opportunity to invest that $6,614 at 8% for 28 years, instead of paying your mortgage, you would have more than $61,000 accumulated. In only three years, your lost future earnings cost is more than $198,000:

Year 1	$ 71,000
Year 2	$ 66,000
Year 3	$ 61,000
Total	$198,000

You can never recapture the lost future earnings cost of $198,000. Why? Because your lender will not give you back the money you paid them in Years 1 through 3. That money is lost forever. This example covers only the first three years of your 30-year mortgage.

Before you learned this critical money principle, you would have thought your total cost for the first three years of this mortgage would have been $19,780 (Year 1 = $6,573 + Year 2 = $6,593 + Year 3 = $6,614). As you now can see, this is not correct. Your real cost is $198,000, not $19,780. If you had the opportunity to invest that $19,780, it would have grown to $198,000 after 30 years.

The following 25 tables show in detail how to arrive at the net lost future earnings cost. Each table will list the mortgage amount, length of mortgage, interest rate, tax bracket, principal balance at the end of the year, annual principal repayment, annual interest, tax savings, net interest cost, total net annual cost (net interest cost plus annual principal repayment), number of years of lost future earnings remaining in the 30-year period, and the lost future earnings cost. I will then summarize the gross lost future earnings cost, and subtract the value of the tax savings invested to arrive at the net lost future earnings cost. To keep these illustrations easy to understand, I have used a fixed-rate mortgage. However, the lost future earnings cost applies to *all* types of mortgages.

Turning to Table 1, when you add up the lost future earnings cost of your mortgage payments for the next 30 years, the gross lost future earnings cost actually totals $1,093,573.

Your tax savings over 30 years are worth $45,963, which will reduce your lost future earnings cost. To further reduce your lost future earnings cost, you should invest these tax savings. If you invested them at 8%, you would have accumulated $232,727. Subtract the $232,727 from the gross lost future earnings cost to arrive at the net lost future earnings cost, which is $860,846.

TABLE 1. Mortgage: $100,000, 30-Years, 8% Interest, Tax Bracket: 28%
Monthly Mortgage Payment: $734 Yearly Mortgage Payment: $8,808

Year	Principal Balance End of Year	Annual Principal Repayment	Annual Interest	28% Tax Savings	Net Interest Cost	Total Net Annual Cost	Number of Years	Lost Future Earnings Cost
1	$99,165	$ 835	$7,970	$2,232	$5,738	$6,573	30	$71,881
5	95,070	1,149	7,656	2,144	5,512	6,661	25	48,893
10	87,725	1,712	7,093	1,986	5,107	6,819	20	33,596
15	76,782	2,551	6,254	1,751	4,503	7,054	15	23,327
20	60,478	3,800	5,005	1,401	3,604	7,404	10	16,434
25	36,188	5,662	3,143	880	2,263	7,925	5	11,807
30	0	8,435	370	104	266	8,701	1	9,423

Gross Lost Future Earnings Cost: $1,093,573
Less Value of Tax Savings Invested: $232,727
Net Lost Future Earnings Cost: $860,846

Let us take a slightly different example. Assume you had a lower interest rate mortgage, perhaps 7%. You are in a very low tax bracket of only 15%. What would your lost future earnings cost be in this case over the 30-year period? Remember, this cost is calculated figuring you could have instead invested your principal and interest payments at 7%.

TABLE 2. Mortgage: $100,000, 30-Years, 7% Interest, Tax Bracket: 15%
Monthly Mortgage Payment: $665 Yearly Mortgage Payment: $7,980

Year	Principal Balance End of Year	Annual Principal Repay-ment	Annual Interest	15% Tax Savings	Net Interest Cost	Total Net Annual Cost	Number of Years	Lost Future Earnings Cost
1	$98,984	$1,016	$6,968	$1,045	$5,923	$6,939	30	$56,320
5	94,132	1,343	6,641	996	5,645	6,988	25	40,009
10	85,812	1,904	6,080	912	5,168	7,072	20	28,562
20	57,300	3,826	4,158	624	3,534	7,360	10	14,791
30	0	7,689	295	44	251	7,940	1	8,514

Gross Lost Future Earnings Cost: $811,648
Less Value of Tax Savings Invested: $86,029
Net Lost Future Earnings Cost: $725,619

Let us look at another example. Assume you are in a high tax bracket of 40%. If you have that same $100,000, 30-year mortgage at 7%, and if you could earn 7% on your alternative investments, what would your gross lost future earnings cost be over 30 years?

Your gross lost future earnings cost would be $811,648. Subtracting the value of your invested tax savings of $229,412 leaves a net lost future earnings cost of $582,236. It is important to point out that when you have a mortgage and are in a higher tax bracket, you will benefit because you will have larger tax deductions.

TABLE 3. Mortgage: $100,000, 30-Years, 7% Interest, Tax Bracket: 40%
Monthly Mortgage Payment: $665 Yearly Mortgage Payment: $7,980

Year	Principal Balance End of Year	Annual Principal Repay-ment	Annual Interest	40% Tax Savings	Net Interest Cost	Total Net Annual Cost	Number of Years	Lost Future Earnings Cost
1	$98,984	$1,016	$6,968	$2,787	$4,181	$5,197	30	$42,181
5	94,132	1,343	6,641	2,656	3,985	5,328	25	30,505
10	85,812	1,904	6,080	2,432	3,648	5,552	20	22,423
20	57,300	3,826	4,158	1,663	2,495	6,321	10	12,703
30	0	7,689	295	118	177	7,866	1	8,435

Gross Lost Future Earnings Cost: $811,648
Less Value of Tax Savings Invested: $229,412
Net Lost Future Earnings Cost: $582,236

What if interest rates rise and you obtain a high-interest mortgage? Let us look at that same $100,000 mortgage at 9% interest, and assume you could also earn 9% in alternative investments. If your tax bracket is only 15%, your gross lost future earnings cost for 30 years is $1,473,059. The tax savings you invested has accumulated to $177,832, subtracting this amount from the gross lost future earnings cost leaves you a net lost future earnings cost of $1,295,227. Due to the higher interest rate of 9% and the low tax bracket of 15% (less tax deductions) your lost future earnings cost is higher than the previous three examples.

TABLE 4. Mortgage: $100,000, 30-Years, 9% Interest, Tax Bracket: 15%
Monthly Mortgage Payment: $805 Yearly Mortgage Payment: $9,660

Year	Principal Balance End of Year	Annual Principal Repay-ment	Annual Interest	15% Tax Savings	Net Interest Cost	Total Net Annual Cost	Number of Years	Lost Future Earnings Cost
1	$99,317	$ 683	$8,972	$1,346	$7,626	$8,309	30	$122,396
5	95,880	978	8,678	1,302	7,376	8,354	25	78,598
10	89,430	1,531	8,124	1,219	6,905	8,436	20	50,693
20	63,518	3,753	5,902	885	5,017	8,770	10	21,498
30	0	9,201	455	68	387	9,588	1	10,487

Gross Lost Future Earnings Cost: $1,473,059
Less Value of Tax Savings Invested: $177,832
Net Lost Future Earnings Cost: $1,295,227

What if you have this same 9% mortgage but your tax bracket is 40%? In this case, the tax break is extremely valuable because you can deduct 40% of all your interest payments from your income taxes. Your gross lost future earnings cost for 30 years is $1,473,059 and your invested tax savings are worth $474,220. Therefore, your net lost future earnings cost is $998,839.

TABLE 5. Mortgage: $100,000, 30-Years, 9% Interest, Tax Bracket: 40%
Monthly Mortgage Payment: $805 Yearly Mortgage Payment: $9,660

Year	Principal Balance End of Year	Annual Principal Repay-ment	Annual Interest	40% Tax Savings	Net Interest Cost	Total Net Annual Cost	Number of Years	Lost Future Earnings Cost
1	$99,317	$ 683	$8,972	$3,589	$5,383	$6,066	30	$89,356
5	95,880	978	8,678	3,471	5,207	6,185	25	58,191
10	89,430	1,531	8,124	3,250	4,874	6,405	20	38,489
20	63,518	3,753	5,902	2,361	3,541	7,294	10	17,880
30	0	9,201	455	182	273	9,474	1	10,363

Gross Lost Future Earnings Cost: $1,473,059
Less Value of Tax Savings Invested: $474,220
Net Lost Future Earnings Cost: $998,839

You probably find the results of these tables fascinating. Most people have never heard of the lost future earnings principle. If they have, they may not have bothered to stop and calculate the lost future earnings cost for their own situation.

Let Us Now Review Larger Mortgages

Once I have shown people the lost future earnings cost on a $100,000 mortgage, many of them are curious to see what happens for even larger mortgages. After all, in many metropolitan areas the average home price is now several hundred thousand dollars. Mortgages of $250,000, $500,000, or even larger are not uncommon today.

As dramatic as the figures are for a $100,000 mortgage, they are even more staggering when you look at the lost future earnings cost for larger mortgages. Let us examine a $250,000 mortgage at 7% interest. Let us assume you are in a low tax bracket of only 15%. If you did not have a mortgage, figure you could invest your money in alternative investments at 7%.

Your gross lost future earnings cost is $2,029,126. Your invested tax savings are worth $215,074 and therefore your net lost future earnings cost would be $1,814,052.

TABLE 6. Mortgage: $250,000, 30-Years, 7% Interest, Tax Bracket: 15%
Monthly Mortgage Payment: $1,663 Yearly Mortgage Payment: $19,956

Year	Principal Balance End of Year	Annual Principal Repay-ment	Annual Interest	15% Tax Savings	Net Interest Cost	Total Net Annual Cost	Number of Years	Lost Future Earnings Cost
1	$247,460	$ 2,540	$17,420	$2,613	$14,807	$17,347	30	$140,797
5	235,329	3,357	16,602	2,490	14,112	17,469	25	100,017
10	214,531	4,760	15,200	2,280	12,920	17,680	20	71,405
20	143,250	9,565	10,394	1,559	8,835	18,400	10	36,978
30	0	19,222	737	110	627	19,849	1	21,284

Gross Lost Future Earnings Cost: $2,029,126
Less Value of Tax Savings Invested: $215,074
Net Lost Future Earnings Cost: $1,814,052

What if you have this same mortgage and you are in the much higher tax bracket of 40%? In this case, your tax deduction would be much more valuable. At the end of 30 years, your total invested tax savings due to the tax deduction would be $573,530 and your net lost future earnings cost would be $1,455,596.

TABLE 7. Mortgage: $250,000, 30-Years, 7% Interest, Tax Bracket: 40%
Monthly Mortgage Payment: $1,663 Yearly Mortgage Payment: $19,956

Year	Principal Balance End of Year	Annual Principal Repay-ment	Annual Interest	40% Tax Savings	Net Interest Cost	Total Net Annual Cost	Number of Years	Lost Future Earnings Cost
1	$247,460	$ 2,540	$17,420	$6,968	$10,452	$12,992	30	$105,450
5	235,329	3,357	16,602	6,641	9,961	13,318	25	76,251
10	214,531	4,760	15,200	6,080	9,120	13,880	20	56,058
20	143,250	9,565	10,394	4,158	6,236	15,801	10	31,755
30	0	19,222	737	295	442	19,664	1	21,086

Gross Lost Future Earnings Cost: $2,029,126
Less Value of Tax Savings Invested: $573,530
Net Lost Future Earnings Cost: $1,455,596

The figures become even more dramatic when we look at a mortgage at the 9% interest rate. Let us assume you have a $250,000 mortgage at 9% interest and that you could also earn 9% on your alternative investments. If you are in the 15% tax bracket, your gross lost future earnings cost would be $3,682,646. Your invested tax savings would amount to $444,581 and therefore your net lost future earnings cost would be a staggering $3,238,065!

TABLE 8. Mortgage: $250,000, 30-Years, 9% Interest, Tax Bracket: 15%
Monthly Mortgage Payment: $2,012 Yearly Mortgage Payment: $24,144

Year	Principal Balance End of Year	Annual Principal Repayment	Annual Interest	15% Tax Savings	Net Interest Cost	Total Net Annual Cost	Number of Years	Lost Future Earnings Cost
1	$248,292	$ 1,708	$22,431	$3,365	$19,066	$20,774	30	$306,013
5	239,700	2,445	21,694	3,254	18,440	20,885	25	196,495
10	223,574	3,828	20,311	3,047	17,264	21,092	20	126,745
20	158,796	9,383	14,755	2,213	12,542	21,925	10	53,746
30	0	23,002	1,137	171	966	23,968	1	26,216

Gross Lost Future Earnings Cost: $3,682,646
Less Value of Tax Savings Invested: $444,581
Net Lost Future Earnings Cost: $3,238,065

What if you were in the 40% tax bracket? With this same $250,000 mortgage at 9% interest, your invested tax savings would be $1,185,551. Subtracting this from your gross lost future earnings cost would net $2,497,095. This example powerfully illustrates just how valuable the mortgage tax deduction is for larger mortgages, and for higher income people.

TABLE 9. Mortgage: $250,000, 30-Years, 9% Interest, Tax Bracket: 40%
Monthly Mortgage Payment: $2,012 Yearly Mortgage Payment: $24,144

Year	Principal Balance End of Year	Annual Principal Repay-ment	Annual Interest	40% Tax Savings	Net Interest Cost	Total Net Annual Cost	Number of Years	Lost Future Earnings Cost
1	$248,292	$ 1,708	$22,431	$8,972	$13,459	$15,167	30	$223,419
5	239,700	2,445	21,694	8,678	13,016	15,461	25	145,463
10	223,574	3,828	20,311	8,124	12,187	16,015	20	96,237
20	158,796	9,383	14,755	5,902	8,853	18,236	10	44,703
30	0	23,002	1,137	455	682	23,684	1	25,906

Gross Lost Future Earnings Cost: $3,682,646
Less Value of Tax Savings Invested: $1,185,551
Net Lost Future Earnings Cost: $2,497,095

It is also important to note that many people may pay even more than 40% in taxes. If you also factor in state taxes, real estate taxes, sales tax, Social Security taxes, Medicare, and workers' compensation taxes you can see that many people pay a large portion of their income to taxes. Although it may seem unfair to pay so much in taxes, we should be thankful and feel fortunate to live in the greatest country in the world—the United States of America! Paying taxes allows us many wonderful benefits, including our freedom.

As you can clearly see, the tax deduction on a mortgage is a very important part of your tax planning. Fortunately, in many states, mortgage interest is tax deductible. This makes the mortgage interest deduction even more valuable, because you can save additional income taxes. Of course, everyone's situation is different and each state is different in the way it treats mortgage interest for tax purposes. For that reason, you should consult with your tax advisor to determine the exact benefit that the mortgage deduction will have for you on your federal and state tax returns.

The most dramatic results of all are seen for people who have large home mortgages, such as $500,000. Let us assume you are in the 15% tax bracket, and had such a mortgage at 7%, and also that you could earn the same 7% on alternative investments. At the end of 30 years, your lost future earnings cost would be $4,058,253. Your invested tax savings on that mortgage would amount to $430,147 and therefore, your net lost future earnings cost would be $3,628,106.

TABLE 10. Mortgage: $500,000, 30-Years, 7% Interest, Tax Bracket: 15%
Monthly Mortgage Payment: $3,327 Yearly Mortgage Payment: $39,924

Year	Principal Balance End of Year	Annual Principal Repayment	Annual Interest	15% Tax Savings	Net Interest Cost	Total Net Annual Cost	Number of Years	Lost Future Earnings Cost
1	$494,921	$ 5,079	$34,839	$5,226	$29,613	$34,692	30	$281,578
5	470,658	6,715	33,203	4,981	28,222	34,937	25	200,029
10	429,062	9,519	30,399	4,560	25,839	35,358	20	142,802
20	286,500	19,130	20,788	3,118	17,670	36,800	10	73,956
30	0	38,445	1,473	221	1,252	39,697	1	42,567

Gross Lost Future Earnings Cost: $4,058,253
Less Value of Tax Savings Invested: $430,147
Net Lost Future Earnings Cost: $3,628,106

If you had this same mortgage and were in the 40% tax bracket, the value of your invested tax savings would be $1,147,059 and you would have a net lost future earnings cost of $2,911,194. A person in the 40% tax bracket would save more than $716,912 as compared with someone who had this same mortgage but was in the 15% tax bracket. Someone who is in a higher tax bracket actually has an advantage over a person who is in a lower tax bracket due to the tax deduction on the mortgage.

TABLE 11. Mortgage: $500,000, 30-Years, 7% Interest, Tax Bracket: 40%
Monthly Mortgage Payment: $3,327 Yearly Mortgage Payment: $39,924

Year	Principal Balance End of Year	Annual Principal Repay-ment	Annual Interest	40% Tax Savings	Net Interest Cost	Total Net Annual Cost	Number of Years	Lost Future Earnings Cost
1	$494,921	$ 5,079	$34,839	$13,936	$20,903	$25,982	30	$210,883
5	470,658	6,715	33,203	13,281	19,922	26,637	25	152,508
10	429,062	9,519	30,399	12,160	18,239	27,758	20	112,107
20	286,500	19,130	20,788	8,315	12,473	31,603	10	63,511
30	0	38,445	1,473	589	884	39,329	1	42,172

Gross Lost Future Earnings Cost: $4,058,253
Less Value of Tax Savings Invested: $1,147,059
Net Lost Future Earnings Cost: $2,911,194

What if you had a $500,000 mortgage and were not fortunate enough to be able to obtain a 7% mortgage? What if you were paying 9% on that mortgage? Let us look at what your net lost future earnings cost would be. If you were in the 15% tax bracket, your gross lost future earnings cost would be $7,365,291. Your invested tax savings would have a value of $889,163 and therefore your net lost future earnings cost would be $6,476,128. As you can see, these numbers can become quite amazing when you factor in the lost future earnings cost principle.

TABLE 12. Mortgage: $500,000, 30-Years, 9% Interest, Tax Bracket: 15%
Monthly Mortgage Payment: $4,023 Yearly Mortgage Payment: $48,276

Year	Principal Balance End of Year	Annual Principal Repay-ment	Annual Interest	15% Tax Savings	Net Interest Cost	Total Net Annual Cost	Number of Years	Lost Future Earnings Cost
1	$496,584	$ 3,416	$44,861	$6,729	$38,132	$41,548	30	$612,026
5	479,401	4,890	43,388	6,508	36,880	41,770	25	392,989
10	447,149	7,656	40,622	6,093	34,529	42,185	20	253,496
20	317,592	18,767	29,511	4,427	25,084	43,851	10	107,494
30	0	46,004	2,273	341	1,932	47,936	1	52,433

Gross Lost Future Earnings Cost: $7,365,291
Less Value of Tax Savings Invested: $889,163
Net Lost Future Earnings Cost: $6,476,128

If you had this same $500,000 mortgage but were in the 40% tax bracket and invested your tax savings, you would have accumulated $2,371,102 over the term of the mortgage. This is an absolutely tremendous tax break. However, your net lost future earnings cost would be a substantial $4,994,189.

TABLE 13. Mortgage: $500,000, 30-Years, 9% Interest, Tax Bracket: 40%
Monthly Mortgage Payment: $4,023 Yearly Mortgage Payment: $48,276

Year	Principal Balance End of Year	Annual Principal Repay-ment	Annual Interest	40% Tax Savings	Net Interest Cost	Total Net Annual Cost	Number of Years	Lost Future Earnings Cost
1	$496,584	$ 3,416	$44,861	$17,945	$26,916	$30,332	30	$446,808
5	479,401	4,890	43,388	17,355	26,033	30,923	25	290,936
10	447,149	7,656	40,622	16,249	24,373	32,029	20	192,467
20	317,592	18,767	29,511	11,804	17,707	36,474	10	89,411
30	0	46,004	2,273	909	1,364	47,368	1	51,702

Gross Lost Future Earnings Cost: $7,365,291
Less Value of Tax Savings Invested: $2,371,102
Net Lost Future Earnings Cost: $4,994,189

How Do I Figure the Lost Future Earnings Cost for a 15-Year Mortgage?

As you have seen from the examples I have presented thus far, it is imperative that you learn as much as possible about mortgages and understand the principle of lost future earnings cost. The figures can be shocking—but they are also very informative and extremely important to understand. It can literally cost you hundreds of thousands of dollars if you make the wrong decisions. These are the most costly mistakes many people make in their entire lifetime.

Some of my clients assume they can minimize or avoid the lost future earnings cost by taking out a 15-year mortgage instead of a 30-year mortgage. While their intentions are good, nothing could be farther from the truth.

One problem with 15-year mortgages is that your tax deductions and your tax savings are much smaller than they are with 30-year mortgages. People who think 15-year mortgages are superior to 30-year mortgages have made another crucial error in judgment because they think the lost future earnings cost lasts for only 15 years. This is absolutely false! Remember, when you make that mortgage payment, you are giving up the principal, net interest, and the potential earnings on the money forever. You will never get that money back. If you had the money, you could invest it and compound your interest. Your money would grow year after year. However, when you give up your money, you give it up forever. You forfeit all the interest you could earn on that money. You give up all the dividends you could earn on that money. You pay a tremendous cost for the rest of your life.

Several tables follow that will clearly demonstrate the differences between a 15-year and 30-year mortgage. Assume you have a 15-year, $100,000 mortgage at 7% interest and you are in the 15% tax bracket. Assume also that you could earn 7% in alternative investments. At the end of

30 years, your gross lost future earnings cost would be $811,648. Your invested tax savings would be only $53,009 because of your lower tax deductions with a 15-year mortgage. Therefore, your net lost future earnings cost would be $758,639.

I figure the lost future earnings cost over 30 years to be consistent with the previous tables, and because you do not give up that money and what it could earn for just 15 years, you give it up forever. Therefore, these 30-year figures are actually conservative. You will really end up losing much more.

TABLE 14. Mortgage: $100,000, 15-Years, 7% Interest, Tax Bracket: 15%
Monthly Mortgage Payment: $899 Yearly Mortgage Payment: $10,788

Year	Principal Balance End of Year	Annual Principal Repayment	Annual Interest	15% Tax Savings	Net Interest Cost	Total Net Annual Cost	Number of Years	Lost Future Earnings Cost
1	$96,090	$ 3,910	$6,876	$1,031	$5,845	$ 9,755	30	$79,176
5	77,413	5,169	5,617	843	4,774	9,943	25	56,928
10	45,393	7,328	3,458	519	2,939	10,267	20	41,466
15	0	10,388	398	60	338	10,726	15	30,558

Gross Lost Future Earnings Cost: $811,648
Less Value of Tax Savings Invested: $53,009
Net Lost Future Earnings Cost: $758,639

What if you had this same mortgage, but you were in the 40% tax bracket? In that case, your total invested tax savings over the 15 years would amount to $141,358 and your net lost future earnings cost would be $670,290.

TABLE 15. Mortgage: $100,000, 15-Years, 7% Interest, Tax Bracket: 40%
Monthly Mortgage Payment: $899 Yearly Mortgage Payment: $10,788

Year	Principal Balance End of Year	Annual Principal Repay-ment	Annual Interest	40% Tax Savings	Net Interest Cost	Total Net Annual Cost	Number of Years	Lost Future Earnings Cost
1	$96,090	$ 3,910	$6,876	$2,750	$4,126	$ 8,036	30	$65,224
5	77,413	5,169	5,617	2,247	3,370	8,539	25	48,889
10	45,393	7,328	3,458	1,383	2,075	9,403	20	37,976
15	0	10,388	398	159	239	10,627	15	30,276

Gross Lost Future Earnings Cost: $811,648
Less Value of Tax Savings Invested: $141,358
Net Lost Future Earnings Cost: $670,290

Now assume you have a 9% interest rate for 15 years with the same $100,000 mortgage and you are in the 15% tax bracket. Your gross lost future earnings cost would be $1,473,059 for a period of 30 years. Your invested tax savings would be worth $116,636 and therefore your net lost future earnings cost would be $1,356,423 over those 30 years.

If you compare this same mortgage amount, tax bracket, and interest rate to the 30-year mortgage, you will see that the 15-year mortgage has a higher net lost future earnings cost. Why? Because your tax deductions are less with a 15-year mortgage. That is the only reason. Everything else is equal. Refer to Table 4 for comparison.

TABLE 16. Mortgage: $100,000, 15-Years, 9% Interest, Tax Bracket: 15%
Monthly Mortgage Payment: $1,014 Yearly Mortgage Payment: $12,168

Year	Principal Balance End of Year	Annual Principal Repay-ment	Annual Interest	15% Tax Savings	Net Interest Cost	Total Net Annual Cost	Number of Years	Lost Future Earnings Cost
1	$96,695	$ 3,305	$8,866	$1,330	$7,536	$10,841	30	$159,694
5	80,068	4,731	7,440	1,116	6,324	11,055	25	104,010
10	48,861	7,408	4,764	715	4,049	11,457	20	68,847
15	0	11,598	573	86	487	12,085	15	46,383

Gross Lost Future Earnings Cost: $1,473,059
Less Value of Tax Savings Invested: $116,636
Net Lost Future Earnings Cost: $1,356,423

If you were instead in the 40% tax bracket and had this same $100,000, 15-year mortgage at 9%, your invested tax savings would be $311,028. Your net lost future earnings cost would therefore be $1,162,031.

TABLE 17. Mortgage: $100,000, 15-Years, 9% Interest, Tax Bracket: 40%
Monthly Mortgage Payment: $1,014 Yearly Mortgage Payment: $12,168

Year	Principal Balance End of Year	Annual Principal Repay-ment	Annual Interest	40% Tax Savings	Net Interest Cost	Total Net Annual Cost	Number of Years	Lost Future Earnings Cost
1	$96,695	$ 3,305	$8,866	$3,546	$5,320	$ 8,625	30	$127,051
5	80,068	4,731	7,440	2,976	4,464	9,195	25	86,510
10	48,861	7,408	4,764	1,905	2,859	10,267	20	61,696
15	0	11,598	573	229	344	11,942	15	45,834

Gross Lost Future Earnings Cost: $1,473,059
Less Value of Tax Savings Invested: $311,028
Net Lost Future Earnings Cost: $1,162,031

The Lost Future Earnings Cost On Larger 15-Year Mortgages

Many people nowadays have 15-year mortgages larger than $100,000. Their thinking on this seems to be, "Since my mortgage is so large, why not pay it off as soon as possible?" While their intention is good, paying off such a large mortgage incurs a tremendous lost future earnings cost, as you will see from the tables in this section.

Assume you have a $250,000 mortgage at 7% interest. If your tax bracket is 15%, your gross lost future earnings cost would be $2,029,126 for 30 years. Remember that we have to use a 30-year period so we can compare the lost future earnings cost with a 30-year mortgage. You will see the only difference is the tax deductions. The tax benefit of your mortgage deduction would be $132,523 and, therefore, your net lost future earnings cost would be $1,896,603.

TABLE 18. Mortgage: $250,000, 15-Years, 7% Interest, Tax Bracket: 15%
Monthly Mortgage Payment: $2,247 Yearly Mortgage Payment: $26,964

Year	Principal Balance End of Year	Annual Principal Repayment	Annual Interest	15% Tax Savings	Net Interest Cost	Total Net Annual Cost	Number of Years	Lost Future Earnings Cost
1	$240,226	$ 9,774	$17,190	$2,579	$14,611	$24,385	30	$197,921
5	193,532	12,922	14,042	2,106	11,936	24,858	25	142,322
10	113,482	18,319	8,646	1,297	7,349	25,668	20	103,666
15	0	25,970	995	149	846	26,816	15	76,397

Gross Lost Future Earnings Cost: $2,029,126
Less Value of Tax Savings Invested: $132,523
Net Lost Future Earnings Cost: $1,896,603

Let us now examine what it would be like to have a $250,000 mortgage, payable in 15 years, with a 7% interest rate, with your personal tax bracket being 40%. Assume also that you could earn 7% on alternative investments. Your gross lost future earnings cost would be $2,029,126. The value of your invested tax savings would be $353,394 and, therefore, your net lost future earnings cost would be $1,675,732.

TABLE 19. Mortgage: $250,000, 15-Years, 7% Interest, Tax Bracket: 40%
Monthly Mortgage Payment: $2,247 Yearly Mortgage Payment: $26,964

Year	Principal Balance End of Year	Annual Principal Repay-ment	Annual Interest	40% Tax Savings	Net Interest Cost	Total Net Annual Cost	Number of Years	Lost Future Earnings Cost
1	$240,226	$ 9,774	$17,190	$6,876	$10,314	$20,088	30	$163,044
5	193,532	12,922	14,042	5,617	8,425	21,347	25	122,221
10	113,482	18,319	8,646	3,458	5,188	23,507	20	94,939
15	0	25,970	995	398	597	26,567	15	75,688

Gross Lost Future Earnings Cost: $2,029,126
Less Value of Tax Savings Invested: $353,394
Net Lost Future Earnings Cost: $1,675,732

Let us look at the scenario with a 9% interest rate. If you could also earn 9% on your alternative investments and if you are in the 15% tax bracket, your gross lost future earnings cost would be $3,682,646. Your invested tax savings would be worth $291,589, so your net lost future earnings cost is $3,391,057!

TABLE 20. Mortgage: $250,000, 15-Years, 9% Interest, Tax Bracket: 15%
Monthly Mortgage Payment: $2,536 Yearly Mortgage Payment: $30,432

Year	Principal Balance End of Year	Annual Principal Repay-ment	Annual Interest	15% Tax Savings	Net Interest Cost	Total Net Annual Cost	Number of Years	Lost Future Earnings Cost
1	$241,737	$ 8,263	$22,165	$3,325	$18,840	$27,103	30	$399,243
5	200,170	11,828	18,600	2,790	15,810	27,638	25	260,030
10	122,152	18,519	11,909	1,786	10,123	28,642	20	172,114
15	0	28,995	1,433	215	1,218	30,213	15	115,959

Gross Lost Future Earnings Cost: $3,682,646
Less Value of Tax Savings Invested: $291,589
Net Lost Future Earnings Cost: $3,391,057

If you had the same $250,000 mortgage but were in the 40% tax bracket, your gross lost future earnings cost would be $3,682,646. Your invested tax savings would be worth considerably more, $777,570, and your net lost future earnings cost would be $2,905,076.

TABLE 21. Mortgage: $250,000, 15-Years, 9% Interest, Tax Bracket: 40%
Monthly Mortgage Payment: $2,536 Yearly Mortgage Payment: $30,432

Year	Principal Balance End of Year	Annual Principal Repay-ment	Annual Interest	40% Tax Savings	Net Interest Cost	Total Net Annual Cost	Number of Years	Lost Future Earnings Cost
1	$241,737	$ 8,263	$22,165	$8,866	$13,299	$21,562	30	$317,621
5	200,170	11,828	18,600	7,440	11,160	22,988	25	216,281
10	122,152	18,519	11,909	4,764	7,145	25,664	20	154,219
15	0	28,995	1,433	573	860	29,855	15	114,585

Gross Lost Future Earnings Cost: $3,682,646
Less Value of Tax Savings Invested: $777,570
Net Lost Future Earnings Cost: $2,905,076

A final set of tables will show what it actually costs you to have a $500,000 home mortgage that is due and payable in 15 years. Assume you are paying 7% interest and that you could earn 7% on your alternative investments. If your tax bracket is 15%, your gross lost future earnings cost is $4,058,253. Your invested tax savings from the mortgage is worth $265,046, so your net lost future earnings cost is $3,793,207.

TABLE 22. Mortgage: $500,000, 15-Years, 7% Interest, Tax Bracket: 15%
Monthly Mortgage Payment: $4,494 Yearly Mortgage Payment: $53,928

Year	Principal Balance End of Year	Annual Principal Repay-ment	Annual Interest	15% Tax Savings	Net Interest Cost	Total Net Annual Cost	Number of Years	Lost Future Earnings Cost
1	$480,451	$19,549	$34,381	$5,157	$29,224	$48,773	30	$395,866
5	387,064	25,845	28,085	4,213	23,872	49,717	25	284,651
10	226,963	36,638	17,291	2,594	14,697	51,335	20	207,329
15	0	51,939	1,990	299	1,691	53,630	15	152,789

Gross Lost Future Earnings Cost: $4,058,253
Less Value of Tax Savings Invested: $265,046
Net Lost Future Earnings Cost: $3,793,207

If you had this same $500,000 mortgage but were in the 40% tax bracket, your gross lost future earnings cost would be the same, but your invested tax savings would have an increased value of $706,789. Therefore, your net lost future earnings cost would be $3,351,464.

TABLE 23. Mortgage: $500,000, 15-Years, 7% Interest, Tax Bracket: 40%
Monthly Mortgage Payment: $4,494 Yearly Mortgage Payment: $53,928

Year	Principal Balance End of Year	Annual Principal Repayment	Annual Interest	40% Tax Savings	Net Interest Cost	Total Net Annual Cost	Number of Years	Lost Future Earnings Cost
1	$480,451	$19,549	$34,381	$13,752	$20,629	$40,178	30	$326,105
5	387,064	25,845	28,085	11,234	16,851	42,696	25	244,452
10	226,963	36,638	17,291	6,917	10,374	47,012	20	189,869
15	0	51,939	1,990	796	1,194	53,133	15	151,373

Gross Lost Future Earnings Cost: $4,058,253
Less Value of Tax Savings Invested: $706,789
Net Lost Future Earnings Cost: $3,351,464

If you have a $500,000 mortgage at 9% and if you could also get 9% on your alternative investments, what would your lost future earnings cost be? Let us assume you are in the 15% tax bracket. Your gross lost future earnings cost would be $7,365,291. The value of your invested tax savings provided by the mortgage interest deduction would be $583,178. Therefore, your net lost future earnings cost would be $6,782,113. This is obviously a fortune!

TABLE 24. Mortgage: $500,000, 15-Years, 9% Interest, Tax Bracket: 15%
Monthly Mortgage Payment: $5,071 Yearly Mortgage Payment: $60,852

Year	Principal Balance End of Year	Annual Principal Repayment	Annual Interest	15% Tax Savings	Net Interest Cost	Total Net Annual Cost	Number of Years	Lost Future Earnings Cost
1	$483,473	$16,527	$44,329	$6,649	$37,680	$54,207	30	$798,500
5	400,340	23,656	37,200	5,580	31,620	55,276	25	520,060
10	244,303	37,038	23,818	3,573	20,245	57,283	20	344,222
15	0	57,990	2,866	430	2,436	60,426	15	231,918

Gross Lost Future Earnings Cost: $7,365,291
Less Value of Tax Savings Invested: $583,178
Net Lost Future Earnings Cost: $6,782,113

What if you had this same $500,000, 15-year mortgage, at the same 9% interest, but were in the 40% tax bracket? Your gross lost future earnings cost would be the same, but the value of your invested mortgage deduction would increase to $1,555,140. You would save more than $1,500,000 by investing your tax savings. Therefore, your net lost future earnings cost would be $5,810,151.

TABLE 25. Mortgage: $500,000, 15-Years, 9% Interest, Tax Bracket: 40%
Monthly Mortgage Payment: $5,071 Yearly Mortgage Payment: $60,852

Year	Principal Balance End of Year	Annual Principal Repay-ment	Annual Interest	40% Tax Savings	Net Interest Cost	Total Net Annual Cost	Number of Years	Lost Future Earnings Cost
1	$483,473	$16,527	$44,329	$17,732	$26,597	$43,124	30	$635,241
5	400,340	23,656	37,200	14,880	22,320	45,976	25	432,561
10	244,303	37,038	23,818	9,527	14,291	51,329	20	308,444
15	0	57,990	2,866	1,146	1,720	59,710	15	229,170

Gross Lost Future Earnings Cost: $7,365,291
Less Value of Tax Savings Invested: $1,555,140
Net Lost Future Earnings Cost: $5,810,151

In the previous 25 tables, I used the same interest rate for both the lost future earnings cost and the mortgage interest rate. You may believe you can earn an even higher rate of return on your investments than what your mortgage interest rate is. If this is true, your lost future earnings cost will increase and so will the real cost of owning your home. The following three tables show the lost future earnings cost at 10% and a mortgage interest rate of 8%.

TABLE 26*. Mortgage: $100,000, 30-Years, 8% Interest, Tax Bracket: 28%
Monthly Mortgage Payment: $734 Yearly Mortgage Payment: $8,808

Year	Principal Balance End of Year	Annual Principal Repayment	Annual Interest	28% Tax Savings	Net Interest Cost	Total Net Annual Cost	Number of Years	Lost Future Earnings Cost at 10%
1	$99,165	$ 835	$7,970	$2,232	$5,738	46,573	30	$130,391
5	95,070	1,149	7,656	2,144	5,512	6,661	25	80,311
10	87,725	1,712	7,093	1,986	5,107	6,819	20	49,970
15	76,782	2,551	6,254	1,751	4,503	7,054	15	31,418
20	60,478	3,800	5,005	1,401	3,604	7,404	10	20,043
25	36,188	5,662	3,143	880	2,263	7,925	5	13,039
30	0	8,435	370	104	266	8,701	1	9,612

Gross Lost Future Earnings Cost: $1,658,666
Less Value of Tax Savings Invested: $364,083
Net Lost Future Earnings Cost: $1,294,583

TABLE 27. Mortgage: $250,000, 30-Years, 8% Interest, Tax Bracket: 28%
Monthly Mortgage Payment: $1,834 Yearly Mortgage Payment: $22,008

Year	Principal Balance End of Year	Annual Principal Repayment	Annual Interest	28% Tax Savings	Net Interest Cost	Total Net Annual Cost	Number of Years	Lost Future Earnings Cost at 10%
1	$247,912	$ 2,088	$19,925	$5,579	$14,346	$16,434	30	$326,008
5	237,675	2,873	19,140	5,359	13,781	16,654	25	199,711
10	219,312	4,280	17,733	4,965	12,768	17,048	20	124,929
15	191,954	6,377	15,636	4,378	11,258	17,635	15	78,545
20	151,195	9,501	12,512	3,503	9,009	18,510	10	50,107
25	90,470	14,154	7,858	2,200	5,658	19,812	5	32,597
30	0	21,088	925	259	666	21,754	1	24,032

Gross Lost Future Earnings Cost: $4,146,664
Less Value of Tax Savings Invested: $910,208
Net Lost Future Earnings Cost: $3,236,456

*Refer to Table 1 for comparison.

TABLE 28. Mortgage: $500,000, 30-Years, 8% Interest, Tax Bracket: 28%
Monthly Mortgage Payment: $3,669 Yearly Mortgage Payment: $44,028

Year	Principal Balance End of Year	Annual Principal Repayment	Annual Interest	28% Tax Savings	Net Interest Cost	Total Net Annual Cost	Number of Years	Lost Future Earnings Cost at 10%
1	$495,823	$ 4,177	$39,849	$11,158	$28,691	$32,868	30	$652,016
5	475,349	5,746	38,280	10,718	27,562	33,308	25	401,593
10	438,624	8,561	35,465	9,930	25,535	34,096	20	249,858
15	383,908	12,754	31,272	8,756	22,516	35,270	15	157,090
20	302,390	19,001	25,025	7,007	18,018	37,019	10	100,212
25	180,941	28,309	15,717	4,401	11,316	39,625	5	65,195
30	0	42,176	1,850	518	1,332	43,508	1	48,064

Gross Lost Future Earnings Cost: $8,293,329
Less Value of Tax Savings Invested: $1,820,415
Net Lost Future Earnings Cost: $6,472,914

You may be shocked at these figures. Even though I am a professional financial planner, I was shocked the first time I calculated these figures. I invite you to go back through this chapter and review all of the tables. I find that people need to study them several times before the full significance of these numbers is understood.

I Have a Different Mortgage and a Different Interest Rate Than All of These Tables

Right now, you might be thinking, these tables are fascinating, but I would like to see the figures for my own mortgage.

Obviously, I cannot include every mortgage amount at every conceivable interest rate. I have taught my strategies for paying off home mortgages in ten years or less without extra payments to a number of financial planners all over the country. These financial planners can take all of your individual mortgage and tax data and generate a detailed, year-by-year printout of your own mortgage. Call my office

(800-729-AIMM) and I will be happy to provide you with the name and address of a financial planner in your area who can perform this service for you.

Economics and Opportunity Cost

Economics is a very complex subject. One important concept in economics is opportunity cost (lost future earnings cost.) You have just learned how this powerful concept can be applied to mortgages.

Why is opportunity cost such an important concept in economics? Because it is usually impossible to get something of value for nothing. There is a cost to obtain a benefit. You must ask yourself the following question: How can I get the maximum return from my money?

In the field of economics there is the concept of the economically irrational individual and the economically rational individual. The person who leaves his/her money at home, stuffed under a mattress, is economically irrational. He/she is paying a tremendous opportunity cost since he/she is giving up all the interest, dividends, and profits he/she could earn on that money. The economically rational individual would invest his/her money to earn the maximum returns; in other words, to achieve opportunity gains.

Conclusion

If you could live mortgage free (or rent free), you would not incur a lost future earnings cost. You could then invest the money that would otherwise have been used for your mortgage (or rent) payments. For most of us, this lost future earnings cost cannot be avoided. However, you can reduce this cost by obtaining a 30-year mortgage, which provides the largest tax deductions. Remember that all three methods of purchasing a house—paying cash, a 15-year mortgage, or a 30-year mortgage—all have identical gross lost future earnings costs. The only difference is the tax deductions. To even further minimize the cost of your home (lost future earnings cost) you should invest your tax savings.

CHAPTER 10

The Investment Mortgage

He is rich enough who owes nothing.
–French proverb

And looks the whole world in the face, for he owes not any man.
–Henry Wadsworth Longfellow, *The Village Blacksmith*

The investment mortgage is an innovative type of home loan that provides

- maximum tax deductions;
- money to pay off your mortgage;
- money for retirement; and
- life insurance coverage.

The investment mortgage accomplishes all of this by combining a specially designed universal life insurance policy with a mortgage. The mortgage is an interest-only loan. With the investment mortgage, there are no principal repayments as there are in a conventional mortgage. Your home will still appreciate with either type of mortgage.

The concept behind the investment mortgage is quite simple. The lending institution provides the borrower with a mortgage, while the life insurance policy provides the borrower with significant cash values to fully pay off the mortgage and offers the potential for additional cash values for retirement. The face value (death benefit) of the life insurance policy will always be at least equal to the mortgage balance. Currently, only 30-year mortgages are available.

Instead of making principal payments, the money accumulates in your life insurance policy. The cash value from your policy grows tax-deferred each year. After 30 years, you will have enough cash value to pay off your mortgage in a single, lump-sum payment. In fact, you should have excess cash value available for retirement or whatever purpose you may choose.

This cash value life insurance policy is portable. In other words, you own it, regardless of who the lender may be. If you were to move and obtain another investment mortgage, you would continue the same life insurance policy with your new mortgage. Should you decide not to continue the investment mortgage, you could continue the life insurance policy by paying the premium.

With this type of mortgage, you have an immediate death benefit. This death benefit could be used to pay off the mortgage or for any other purpose if the insured dies.

However, let me caution you about two critical points: (1) be sure the life insurance policy is guaranteed to accumulate enough cash value to be able to pay off your mortgage after 30 years; and (2) you want to ensure that the life insurance company who underwrites the policy is financially sound.

It is important to note that the investment mortgage has been very successful in Western Europe and the United Kingdom. More than 60% of all residential mortgages made in the United Kingdom are based on this concept, which in

England is called the "endowment mortgage." This concept has been further refined for the American market. Because of the more favorable tax treatment of home mortgage interest and the tax-deferred growth on cash value life insurance, this mortgage makes even more sense here in America than it does in England. Therefore, it is expected to become popular as more and more consumers learn of its availability.

For many years, Americans looked at their homes as great investments. It seemed that real estate prices went only one way—up. Americans were happy to pay their mortgages because they believed that their homes were increasing in value each year. However, recent economic events have shown that real estate prices can stay level or even go down. Can you really count on your home to provide you with significant security when you retire? The investment mortgage has the potential to provide money for retirement.

A major advantage of the investment mortgage is that it is a forced savings. You may want to consider this type of mortgage if you have difficulty saving money. Furthermore, if you incur financial hardship you may not be able to save any money, but you will make every effort to make your mortgage payments. When you do make mortgage payments with the investment mortgage, you will accumulate money in your cash value life insurance policy.

The easiest way to explain how the investment mortgage works is through an illustration. Let us assume for the moment that you are a prospective borrower. In the following illustration, I will compare two mortgage options: (1) the conventional mortgage and (2) the investment mortgage.

	Conventional Mortgage	**Investment Mortgage**
Amount of Mortgage	$200,000	$200,000
Term of Mortgage	30 Years	30 Years
Type of Mortgage	ARM	ARM
Initial Interest Rate	6.125%	6.125%
Initial Payment	$1,215.22	$1,306.62
Policy Cash Value* (after 30 years)	-0-	$251,095.46
Principal Repayment	Paid by mortgage payments	$200,000— Paid by policy cash value
Policy Net Cash Value (after 30 years)	-0-	$51,095.46
Mortgage Paid in Event of Death	No	Yes

* For illustration purposes, the universal life policy is based on 6.5% interest rate, male, age 40, nonsmoker.

Each option provides the same mortgage amount, as well as the same interest rate. Each mortgage is for 30 years. However, that is where the similarities end.

In this illustration, the investment mortgage creates a cash value of $251,095.46. This money is from the universal life policy's cash values that have accumulated over 30 years. At the end of the mortgage term, the borrower withdraws $200,000 from the universal life policy to repay the lender the original $200,000 mortgage. Not only is there sufficient money to repay the mortgage, but there is an excess accumulation of $51,095 which can be used for retirement or any other purpose. Should the borrower die, even after only one mortgage payment, the mortgage would be fully repaid. If there was any excess death benefit in the policy—beyond what is required to pay off the mortgage—it would be paid to the designated beneficiary income tax free.

Two key elements make the investment mortgage very appealing. One of these elements is the tax treatment that exists for mortgage interest. The investment mortgage is an interest-only loan which provides you with maximum tax deductions every year. The second key element is that the earnings on the cash value from the life insurance policy are tax deferred until the time the cash is withdrawn. This means the cash value that accumulates within the life insurance policy is untaxed until the money is withdrawn. This tax-deferred accumulation can become quite significant. If you withdraw money from your cash value life insurance policy through policy loans, you incur no income tax on the money received. I recommend that you consult with your tax advisor or financial planner for details on the current tax laws regarding policy loans. Remember, you always have the option to use whatever cash value you have accumulated to reduce or completely pay off your mortgage before 30 years.

Tax Benefits of a Conventional Mortgage Compared with the Investment Mortgage

Conventional mortgages require monthly payments, which include a combination of principal and interest. During the term of the mortgage, the relative proportions of principal and interest will change. In the first ten years of a 30-year conventional mortgage, the majority of your monthly payment is used to pay interest and the remainder is used to reduce the principal balance. The payment amount is based on full amortization of the mortgage during its term. If you have a 30-year mortgage you will amortize a small amount of this principal over each of the 30 years until it is finally paid off. The interest you pay each month is calculated on the outstanding principal balance of the mortgage. As this outstanding principal is reduced, your home's equity will increase.

With a conventional mortgage the borrower loses tax deductions each year. This is because a smaller amount of each payment goes toward interest. As the years go by, the interest deduction continues to disappear. This results in an increasing after-tax cost every year. With a conventional mortgage you might receive a $15,000 tax deduction in the first year of your mortgage and only a $2,000 tax deduction in the last year.

In contrast to a conventional mortgage, the investment mortgage does not amortize, which means there is no monthly reduction of principal. Since the interest payment remains level for the length of the mortgage, you get the same maximum tax deduction on your interest in the thirtieth year of the mortgage as you received in the first year of the mortgage. Using our previous example, you would receive the same $15,000 tax deduction every year of the 30-year time frame. Obviously, this income tax deduction is extremely valuable. For many people the home mortgage interest deduction is the largest income tax deduction they have. See your tax advisor regarding the phase-out rules for exemptions and itemized deductions for high income earners.

Unlike a conventional mortgage, with the investment mortgage the borrower ends up with money at the end of the term because of the life insurance policy's cash value. Using our previous illustration, with the investment mortgage you will have a net cash value of $51,000 after you pay off your mortgage. The investment mortgage payment is usually a little higher than a conventional mortgage payment. This is due to the life insurance premium, which is part of the investment mortgage monthly payment. The conventional monthly mortgage payment is $1,215 and the investment mortgage is $1,307. The difference in mortgage payments is $92 every month which you could invest in an alternative investment. If you can maintain a strict investment discipline of $92 each and every month for 30 years, you would have accumulated $164,000 ($92 per month x 12 months = $1,104 per year invested at 9%). This is $113,000 more than the $51,000 from the cash value of the investment mortgage. However, you need to remember that the investment mortgage provides larger tax deductions as well as life insurance protection (death benefit).

Where Can You Get the Investment Mortgage?

There are lenders throughout the United States that make these mortgages available. Investment Mortgage Corporation, the creator of the Money Back Home Loan™, has a network of lenders that provides non-amortizing, interest-only mortgages for borrowers. They also have quality life insurance companies that provide the life insurance element of this type of loan.*

Why would a lender be willing to defer repayment of principal for a period as long as 30 years? There are several reasons. The investment mortgage has less risk than a conventional mortgage because it is fully secured by the home and the cash value of the policy is also pledged as additional security to the lender. In addition, if the borrower dies at any time during the repayment period the lender is guaranteed to be repaid in full. Finally, the lender earns more money because it receives the full interest payment every month for the full 30 years.

Let us look at an example of how the investment mortgage could benefit homeowners during their lives. Maria

---

* If you cannot find an investment mortgage lender in your area, call the American Institute for Money Management, Inc, 800-729-AIMM, for a referral.

and Travis bought their first house, a three-bedroom, two-bathroom ranch. The purchase price, $200,000, seemed like a fortune to them at the time. As first-time buyers, they had to scrape together every penny to come up with a down payment. After many hours of interviewing different lenders, the couple decided to obtain the investment mortgage.

Several years later, Maria and Travis were doing very well financially. Travis was a junior executive at his firm and Maria had started a home-based business that was progressing nicely. They had outgrown their present home; Maria's home-based business was taking up one bedroom and their two daughters were tired of sharing the third bedroom. It was time to move.

They decided to sell their house and began searching for a larger home. They found a perfect house, but the price was $400,000. Travis and Maria were not sure they could afford it, but they knew they had to move. Maria and Travis also realized that real estate prices were not going down. The house that costs $400,000 today may well be worth $420,000 or more next year. They decided to buy it.

Maria and Travis had watched the cash value build up in their investment mortgage. They were pleased with how much cash value they had accumulated and especially liked the fact that they were still getting the maximum tax deductions from their mortgage interest. These tax deductions did not decrease during the years they lived in their home. They decided to use the same method to finance their next home.

After the sale of their home, the couple applied their available cash of $107,500 toward the down payment for the new house. They financed the balance of the purchase price of $400,000 with another investment mortgage of $292,500. The insurance policy continued with the new mortgage. In addition to all the money they had made from the sale of their first home, they had also built up another $17,500 in cash values from their insurance policy. They realized that as this money grew each year, it would reduce and eventually completely pay off their new $292,500 mortgage in approximately 20 years. In addition, both Maria and Travis felt considerable peace of mind knowing that their new mortgage would be completely paid off in the event of Travis' death.

Travis became a senior executive at his firm and Maria's home-based business thrived. Their friends who had conventional mortgages were losing their tax deductions each year. Some of them had almost no mortgage interest deductions left and therefore paid higher income taxes. Maria and Travis continued to benefit from the same tax deductions each year.

Due to rising real estate prices, Maria and Travis' home soared in value. As they started to look forward to retirement, the couple realized their home was worth more than $800,000. The investment mortgage they had obtained many years earlier completely paid off their mortgage. They were delighted that they owned their home free and clear, and also were very excited about the $140,000 in remaining cash values from the life insurance policy that the investment mortgage provided. They were free to use this cash in any way they chose. They were happily looking forward to a financially secure retirement. Maria and Travis were completely debt free.

Interest-Only Mortgages Without the Life Insurance

There are interest-only mortgages available without the life insurance feature. These mortgages do not reduce or repay principal. You pay only interest to the lender. At the end of the mortgage term, the original principal—the total amount of the mortgage—must be repaid to the lender. It is critical the borrower has enough money through savings, investments, or some other means to pay off the debt. If he/she does not have enough money to repay the lender, the borrower has the option of refinancing his/her mortgage. He/she must be able to qualify financially to receive another mortgage. The problem that can occur in this situation is if the borrower cannot qualify for a new mortgage. An interest-only mortgage should only be considered if you are positive that you will have the money or resources to repay the mortgage.

CHAPTER

11

Secrets of Mortgage Prepayment Strategies and Biweekly Mortgages

A mortgage casts a shadow on the sunniest field.
–R. G. Ingersoll, *About Farming in Illinois*
Loans and debts make worries and frets.
–W. G. Benham, *Proverbs*

In general, I believe the best course of action is not to make prepayments on your mortgage. First, when you make prepayments you will not save any money on interest charges. Remember, your prepayments could have been invested in alternative investments, such as stocks, mutual funds, bonds, or savings accounts where they could have earned interest, dividends, and capital gains.

Second, by prepaying your mortgage, you could receive lower tax deductions which may cause you to pay more in income taxes. These lost tax deductions will increase the cost of your mortgage. The higher the tax bracket you are in, the more important the tax deductions are. For example, if you have an 8% mortgage and are in the 15% tax bracket, your tax deductions will reduce your mortgage interest cost to 6.8%. However, if you are in the 40% tax bracket, and have the same 8% mortgage, your tax deductions will reduce your mortgage interest cost to only 4.8%.

Third, the tax savings you forfeit from the lost tax deductions could have been invested and would have accumulated to a substantial amount of money over many years. Therefore, these lost tax deductions will increase your lost future earnings* cost.

Fourth, a mortgage is one of the least expensive methods of borrowing money. Therefore, instead of making prepayments, you may be better off investing your money in alternative investments that could earn a higher return than the cost of your mortgage.

Fifth, when you make prepayments, you are using today's expensive dollars instead of paying with tomorrow's cheaper dollars. In other words, you will not be using inflation to your advantage when you make prepayments.

Sixth, before you make any mortgage prepayments, you should pay off all your high nondeductible interest debts, such as credit cards or other consumer loans, before starting to prepay your low tax-deductible mortgage.

Seventh, even though you are quickly building up equity, by making prepayments you are losing control of your money. Should you ever need to use this equity, you would have to refinance or obtain a home equity loan. You would then incur additional interest charges and/or fees just to access your own money.

Eighth, invest in a retirement plan, such as a 401(k), IRA, or 403(b), before making mortgage prepayments. This

---

* *Lost future earnings* and *loss of future earnings* are interchangeable. In this book, we will use lost future earnings.

is especially true if you have a 401(k) and your employer will match any of your contributions. These tax deferral retirement plans will maximize your current tax savings.

Finally, believe it or not, your home mortgage may actually help protect you from lawsuits. If someone feels that he/she has a legitimate reason to file a lawsuit, his/her lawyer can learn important information about your financial situation, such as how much real estate you own and the amount of the mortgage against each property. By making prepayments you are eliminating your debt and quickly building up equity. Should the lawyer discover that you own your home free and clear or your home is almost paid off, you could be more susceptible to a lawsuit because of the equity in your home. If a lawsuit is filed against you and you lose, the court may require you to sell your home or take out a loan to pay the judgment. Therefore, if you have a mortgage, it may not be as appealing to file a lawsuit against you. Since you have this debt on your home, it could be difficult to collect any money.

Many states have laws that protect your home against such lawsuits. The amount of the homestead exemption varies from state to state. I recommend that you consult with your attorney to find out what the law is in the state(s) where you own real estate.

Let us look at an example of how prepaying a mortgage will effect your cost of the mortgage. We will assume you have a $100,000, 30-year mortgage at an 8% interest rate. Your tax bracket is 31%. Your goal is to pay off your mortgage in 15 years. To accomplish your goal, you will need an extra $221 every month in addition to your regular mortgage payment. One option would be to make mortgage prepayments of $221 a month for 15 years. Another option would be to invest $221 every month in alternative investments. Assuming an 8% return, after 15 years, you would have accumulated $76,782, which would then be enough to pay off your mortgage in one lump sum payment. Let us look at the results after we take into account the lost future earnings cost on your money over a 30-year period and the tax deductions for each option. For a complete comparison, I have also included paying your 30-year mortgage for its full term.

	Prepaid Mortgage—Mortgage Prepayment $221 a Month		Prepaid Mortgage—Lump Sum Payment $76,782 15th Year		30-Year Mortgage—Paid for Its Full Term	
	Cost	LFE* Cost	Cost	LFE* Cost	Cost	LFE* Cost
Total Interest and Principal Paid	$172,167	$1,093,573	$209,371	$1,093,573	$264,155	$1,093,573
Less: Cumulative Taxes Saved	- 22,372	- 164,058†	- 33,905	- 220,144†	- 50,888	- 257,662†
Net Cost	$149,795	$ 929,515	$175,466	$ 873,429	$213,267	$ 835,912

*LFE means Lost Future Earnings
†Value of tax savings that were invested

Your first observation would be to assume that the $221 a month prepayment method is the least costly. However, you must consider three important factors to arrive at the real cost of financing your mortgage: (1) remember you did not save any interest charges because you could have invested the $221 prepayments in alternative investments; (2) this method provides the lowest tax savings; and (3) your lost future earnings cost on your money is the highest using this method because of the lost tax deductions.

If there were no tax deductions allowed on your mortgage then your real cost of the house would be identical in all three situations. In this example, your gross lost future earnings cost would be $1,093,573 for each method. After you subtract your invested tax savings, you would then arrive at your net lost future earnings cost.

As you can see, the most costly method of financing your mortgage would be to make prepayments. The least costly method would be to pay your 30-year mortgage for its full term. If you still want to pay off your house in 15 years, your best option would be to accumulate enough money in alternative investments so that you could make one lump sum payment in Year 15.

If you are not disciplined enough to save or invest money, making prepayments to pay off your mortgage may make sense. You may have had a bad experience investing your money and do not want to take a chance with alternative investments. You also may feel that you do not want to work with a financial planner. If paying down your mortgage will make you feel less stressful, then making prepayments should be considered. After all, a home is one of the few investments you can enjoy and use on a daily basis.

Investing your money in mortgage prepayments can be very safe. You will not risk this money which could be lost in other investments, such as stocks, mutual funds, other real estate, limited partnerships, or gold. Prepaying a mortgage is equivalent to investing pre-tax, so this strategy will make more sense for low tax bracket homeowners. For example, if you have a 10% mortgage and your tax bracket is 15%, you will have a net savings of 8½% by prepaying your mortgage. Unless you can find a safe, after-tax 8½% return or higher on your investment, prepaying your mortgage may make sense. If you have any savings or investments that are earning lower than 8½% return, you could use that money to prepay your mortgage.

Finally, if you cannot find alternative investments that will earn you a higher rate of return than the interest you are paying on your mortgage, it then makes sense to make prepayments or biweekly payments to reduce or pay off your mortgage. For example, if the after-tax cost of your mortgage is 9% and all you can earn on alternative investments is 7%, it would make financial sense to use whatever money you have to reduce and eventually pay off your mortgage. However, you need to realize that these conditions are not the norm. You should be able to find investments that will have higher rates of return than your mortgage interest rate. Then, when you have enough money accumulated from your investments to completely pay off your mortgage, you can accomplish this by making one final lump-sum payment.

Remember, the key to successful investing is diversification. If you decide to pay down or pay off your mortgage, make sure you have other savings and investments besides the equity in your home. Real estate prices can go down, which in turn, would cause your equity to decrease.

Mortgage Prepayment Strategies

Now I will show you four strategies for making prepayments, including the advantages and disadvantages of each. The first strategy is what I call the "Next Principal Payment." As simple as this strategy is, millions of American homeowners have never thought of it, nor have they ever used it. To learn how to use the Next Principal Payment strategy you must first review the amortization schedule for your mortgage. If you do not have such a schedule, ask your lender for one.

Payments for the duration of your mortgage are listed on this schedule. Also included on the amortization schedule is your total monthly payment, the amount that goes toward principal, the amount that pays interest, and the remaining principal balance. You should notice from looking at your amortization schedule that as the principal portion of your payment increases (increasing your equity) the interest portion decreases. This is the secret to the effectiveness of the Next Principal Payment strategy.

Here is how to use the Next Principal Payment strategy: Every time you write out a check for your monthly mortgage payment, add an extra payment for next month's principal. Let us look at an example to see how this works in actual practice. We will say that your monthly mortgage payment is $800. Of that payment, $750 is for interest and $50 is for principal. When you write your check, make it out for $850 instead of $800. By doing so, you will be paying this month's mortgage interest and principal—and you will be prepaying next month's principal. Therefore, the lender will not be able to charge you interest on that prepaid principal portion. When you prepay next month's principal, state the exact amount of prepayment on your check. If you have to send in a payment coupon, also note the amount of prepayment on the coupon. By doing this, you will be assured that you are properly credited for this prepayment of principal.

Occasionally, ask your lender to recompute your amortization schedule. This will show you just how quickly you are paying off your mortgage. In fact, you will see that you are eliminating two months at a time. If you do this every month, you can pay off your mortgage in roughly one-half the time it would ordinarily have taken.

To recompute your amortization schedule, you can assume you will continue making these double principal payments for the duration of your mortgage. However, some lenders are not able to recompute an amortization schedule based on that assumption. If this is the case with your lender, just assume you will make one year of double principal payments and have the rest of your amortization schedule recomputed based on that one year.

If you decide to continue this process for a second year, have your amortization schedule again recomputed. While it will not be to the exact penny, each year's schedule will be fairly accurate. This may seem like a lot of work, but it is not. Many lenders, mortgage brokers, and financial planners have computer programs that can produce an amortization schedule in just a few minutes. You do not even have to go to their office. In many cases, you can call in your request and have them fax you the new amortization schedule. If that is not possible, the lender can always mail it to you.

The Next Principal Payment strategy sounds exciting to many people. However, there are a couple of drawbacks to this strategy that you should be aware of. First, you will not accomplish very much if you only do this for two or three months. You need to make these double principal payments every month, month after month, year after year.

Second, do not underestimate the difficulty of this strategy. You may be saying to yourself, "No problem. I have to send in my mortgage payment anyway. What is so difficult about adding a few extra dollars to it?" In the early years of the mortgage, you are only adding a small amount toward the principal each month. However, as your mortgage gets paid down, the portion of your monthly payment going to principal increases dramatically. At first, you may only have to add $50 a month to make an extra principal payment. However, in later years, you may have to add $1,000 a month or more to your payments to continue this strategy. It is difficult to anticipate exactly what your financial situation will be in the future. You have to ask yourself two questions: Will my income grow sufficiently to be able to afford these increasingly larger payments? and Do I want to continue making them? The savings on your interest charges can be substantial if you can utilize this strategy. This strategy might actually cut your interest charges and the duration of your mortgage in half.

If you cannot follow your amortization schedule, consider the "Extra Principal Prepayment" strategy. To use this strategy, first analyze your monthly budget. Determine how much money you can easily and comfortably set aside for a regular monthly prepayment. Even making a small monthly prepayment could be very helpful in rapidly paying down your mortgage. Once you have made a commitment to set aside a certain amount of money for prepayment of principal, do it every month. Discipline is the secret to making this work.

If your income increases, you may want to increase the amount you pay each month for principal prepayment. You might start by making prepayments of only $100 a month, but after a couple of years and as your income increases, you can afford to set aside $250 a month for prepayments.

Here are some general guidelines that you can use to determine the size of your prepayments. The amount of your outstanding principal balance (as well as the interest rate) will have an affect as to when your mortgage will be paid off. Assume you have a 30-year mortgage. If you want to pay it off in approximately 20 to 25 years, increase your monthly mortgage payments by 10%. For example, if your payment is $800 per month, send in $880 ($800 x 10%) every month.

If you want to pay off your 30-year mortgage in approximately 15 to 20 years, increase your monthly mortgage payments by 20%. If your payment is $800 per month, send in $960 each month.

If you want to pay off your 30-year mortgage in approximately 10 to 15 years, increase your monthly mortgage payments by 50%. If your payment is $800 per month, send in $1,200. Many financial planners can help you determine how many years it will take to pay off your mortgage based on the amount of your prepayment.

Here is the third strategy for determining the amount of your prepayment. I call it the "1/12th Principle Payment" strategy. If you look back at your amortization schedule, you will notice that your principal payments are not equal each month. The portion of your payment going to principal increases each month.

To determine how much you may want to prepay each month, take the next 12 scheduled principal payments, add them up, and divide by 12. Take this $^1/_{12}$ figure and add it to your regular mortgage payment each month. Do this calculation once a year. For example, if your scheduled annual principal payments are $1,200, you would divide this by 12, which equals $100. Each month $100 would be the additional amount you would pay as your prepayment.

The fourth strategy is the "Occasional Principal Prepayment" strategy. If you are going to prepay your principal, I strongly recommend that you do so on a regular basis. Get into the habit of doing this monthly to achieve the maximum benefit. However, for various reasons, some people cannot make a regular extra payment each month. If you are one of these people, you can make occasional prepayments of principal and still benefit considerably by reducing the length of your mortgage and the amount of interest you will ultimately have to pay.

Whether you pay $50, $100, or a few thousand dollars at the end of the year toward paying down your principal, over a period of time these occasional prepayments can result in tremendous savings. Whenever you have extra money ask yourself, "How much of this can I use toward paying down the principal on my mortgage?"

By implementing this strategy, you will find that you will be able to pay down your mortgage in much less time than you ever thought possible. You may also start finding creative ways of saving money. Each time you save some money (for example, buying something on sale, putting off a purchase, buying the less expensive item, buying something used) you can apply the money you have saved toward an occasional principal prepayment. Before you know it, your large mortgage debt will be a small one. You will start to see the reality that you are becoming mortgage free.

There is a point when you might want to consider stopping or reducing your prepayments. You might want to think of this as a point of diminishing returns. After a certain amount of time, you will notice that your prepayments are not saving you as much interest as the earlier prepayments.

The Biweekly Mortgage

You have just learned four prepayment strategies to become mortgage free:

- Next Principal Payment;
- Extra Principal Prepayment;
- 1/12th Principal Prepayment; and
- Occasional Principal Prepayment.

The biweekly program is another option you can use to make extra payments. Seminars have been developed around this concept. I know of a biweekly mortgage service company that charges $595 just to teach people about the biweekly mortgage. Some of these companies charge several hundred dollars in additional fees to sign you up for their program. It is a simple concept that you can learn yourself. You should not have to pay hundreds of dollars for this service. Check with your own lending institution to find out if this service is available at no cost to you.

Here is how the biweekly program works. The biweekly mortgage service company collects an amount equal to half a monthly mortgage payment every two weeks. Since a year has 52 weeks, you end up making 26 payments. This is equivalent to 13 monthly mortgage payments, which would be one extra monthly payment each year. This will result in paying off your mortgage early.

You can make this strategy even more effective by making additional prepayments on your mortgage. Making these extra principal payments, combined with a biweekly mortgage, will help you pay off your mortgage very quickly.

Be aware of the fine print in the mortgage servicing documents. It may state that the mortgage service company is not to be held responsible or liable for any late fees or penalties. In other words, if the service company does not pay your mortgage on time, you have to pay the late fee.

If you believe the biweekly mortgage—or any of the four prepayment methods—is a viable strategy, be sure your mortgage does not prohibit or penalize principal prepayments. If your mortgage has a prepayment penalty, find out the date it expires. You can start your biweekly or other prepayment program after the expiration date. If it does prohibit prepayments, the biweekly mortgage or other prepayment strategies may not work for you.

Remember, the biweekly mortgage service company will charge you a fee just to send the payments to your lender once a month. You should not have to pay a fee since you can easily make these payments yourself. I urge extreme caution in selecting any biweekly mortgage service company. Make sure that you only work with the most established and reputable companies.

Conclusion

There are situations when making prepayments may make sense. There is no right or wrong way to make these principal prepayments. The secret is to find a strategy that makes sense to you and that you are comfortable with. Once you have found the strategy that works for you, stay with it. However, keep in mind you are foregoing the option to invest in alternative investments, plus, you are losing valuable tax deductions when you make principal prepayments.

Consider all of the options that are available to you. My goal is to give you a number of choices for paying off your mortgage early. In the next chapter you will learn how to become mortgage free in ten years or less, without extra payments.

CHAPTER 12

Forty-Two Strategies to Become Mortgage Free

Out of debt, out of danger.
–John Ray, *English Proverbs*
Rather go to bed supperless than rise in debt.
–Benjamin Franklin, *Poor Richard's Almanac*

The following proven strategies will put you in the position to pay off your mortgage without making prepayments or losing tax deductions. These strategies will show you how to accumulate money so that if or when you decide to pay off your mortgage, you can accomplish this with a single lump-sum payment. This makes the most financial sense because you can take full advantage of your tax deductions each year until you pay off your mortgage.

You do not have to use all of these strategies. If you use just one or two, you will be able to pay off your home mortgage very quickly. If you can apply three or four strategies, you will pay off your mortgage faster than you can imagine. Do not discard or ignore a strategy just because it does not fit into your present personal situation. Learn all of the strategies. A strategy that may not work for you today might become important tomorrow. For example, you may not have a 401(k) plan, so you might think you could ignore learning that strategy. However, your employer may start a 401(k) program. In this case, your knowledge of the strategies using retirement plans would be very important. As you read through the following strategies, keep an open mind as to how you might use each strategy today as well as in the future.

A very important point to remember is this: The longer you wait, the longer it will take you to become mortgage free. If you had learned and applied these strategies ten years ago, you would be mortgage free today, or you would have accumulated enough money to be able to pay off your home mortgage whenever you choose. Carefully read all of these strategies, pick two or three of your favorites, and start applying them today.

Let us now look at the 42 strategies you can apply to pay off your mortgage in ten years or less without extra payments.

Mappa Strategy Number 1

Open a "Mortgage-Free" Checking Account

I have found that many of the people who are successful at paying off their home mortgage in ten years or less have opened a special mortgage-free checking account. I would strongly encourage you to set up such an account for yourself. This special account will help you focus on your objective of becoming mortgage free. To achieve this objective, you need to accumulate enough money to pay off your home in a single lump-sum payment.

There are two reasons to establish a mortgage-free checking account. The first is to deposit money so that you can invest it where it will accumulate to help pay off your mortgage. By depositing the money into the mortgage-free checking account, the chances of you spending it, instead of investing it, are greatly reduced.

The second reason for having this special mortgage-free checking account is to maintain accurate records of all deposits and investments. Whenever you have any money to invest, deposit it into your special account with the notation of where it came from, and then invest it. For example, let us say you deposit your $5,000 bonus from work into your special checking account. You decide a growth mutual fund is an excellent investment to help you accumulate money to reach your objective of becoming mortgage free. Seven years later you ask yourself, "Where did I get my original $5,000 to invest in this growth mutual fund?" All you need to do is look in your mortgage-free checking account register to find the answer. You had made a notation that the $5,000 was a bonus from work. This information may also be important to you someday if you need it for tax purposes.

You need to see this account as being exclusively dedicated to paying off your home mortgage. Giving it the appropriate name is a good start. You may want to call it your "Mortgage-Free" account. Some banks will allow you to label your checks the "John Doe Mortgage-Free Account." I recommend that you order business-size checks, which come in a three-ring binder with three checks on each page. There is plenty of writing space for deposit information, notes, and any remarks you believe are important for future reference.

You should not use the money in your special account for any purpose other than for investments which will accomplish your mortgage-free objective. Do not use the money in your mortgage-free checking account to pay the phone bill, the electric bill, buy new clothes, a new car, or a CD player. These are all important items, but you should find some other source of money for these expenses and purchases. Use your personal checking account to pay for these expenditures.

Mappa Strategy Number 2
Invest the Money Instead of Making Extra Mortgage Payments

As you've learned, making mortgage prepayments usually is not to your advantage since you lose valuable tax deductions. You can generally invest the money in alternative investments which could earn a higher rate of return than the cost of your mortgage. If you currently are making or plan to make prepayments, you should invest the money instead. For example, instead of making a prepayment of $200 every month, if you invested this money at 9%, in ten years it would grow to $39,744. This money could then be used to reduce your mortgage.

Mappa Strategy Number 3
If Interest Rates Decline, Refinance Your Home and Invest the Savings

One of the smartest strategies you can apply during times of declining interest rates is to refinance your mortgage. By taking advantage of these lower rates, you will have lower monthly payments. You can then invest the money you save from these lower mortgage payments every month. For example, if you have a $150,000, 30-year fixed-rate mortgage at 10%, your monthly payments will be $1,316. If you can refinance to 8%, your monthly payments will decrease to $1,101. You can invest the difference of $215 every month ($2,580 yearly). If you can earn 8% on your money, in ten years you will have accumulated $40,351. To further increase your savings, you may want to consider an adjustable-rate mortgage instead of a fixed-rate mortgage. When fixed-rates are at 8% it is often possible to get an adjustable-rate at 6%. The introductory rate for the first six months or one year might be only 5%.

Mappa Strategy Number 4

Invest the Tax Savings from the Mortgage Interest Deduction on Your Home

As you know, the interest paid on a home mortgage is tax deductible for most homeowners. You should also know by now that a 30-year mortgage gives you the largest tax deductions and, therefore, the largest tax savings. Let us say that your mortgage deduction saves you $3,000 in taxes. We will assume the tax savings are $3,000 every year to make this calculation easy to understand. What will you do with that $3,000 savings? If you simply invest it each year at 9%, after 10 years you will have accumulated $49,680, which you can use to pay down your mortgage. In this example, if your mortgage is $100,000, this one strategy alone could pay close to 50% of your mortgage. I have found very few people take advantage of investing their tax savings. They simply spend the money rather than using it to help pay off their mortgage. If you cannot save all of the tax savings, try to invest at least some of them.

Mappa Strategy Number 5

Invest the Tax Savings from Your 401(k) or IRA

Let us say that you are putting $4,000 a year into your 401(k) or IRA ($2,000 each for you and your working spouse; and assuming your IRA is tax deductible). If you are in the 33% tax bracket, you are currently saving $1,320 a year in taxes. If you invested this $1,320 every year for 10 years at 9%, you would have accumulated $21,859 which could be used toward paying off your home mortgage. The combination of this idea with the strategies you have already learned in this chapter could easily help you pay off your home mortgage in 10 years or less.

Mappa Strategy Number 6

Change Your 15-Year Mortgage to a 30-Year Mortgage

Chapter 8 explained all of the advantages of 30-year mortgages over 15-year mortgages. One major advantage is that your monthly mortgage payment will be less. For a $100,000, 15-year mortgage at 8%, the payments will be $955. For the same 30-year mortgage, the monthly payments will only be $734. You can invest the difference of $221 every month. Over the course of a year, this is $2,652 in additional money you would have to invest. If you invested this $2,652 at 8% for 10 years, your investment would be worth $41,477. You can also invest the additional tax savings a 30-year mortgage will provide. By investing the difference in mortgage payments and the additional tax savings, you will accumulate a substantial amount of money toward reaching your goal of becoming mortgage free.

Mappa Strategy Number 7

Buy a Less Expensive House

You are in the market for a new house. You found two homes that are affordable and you would be happy with either one. One house is selling for $300,000 and the other asking price is $260,000. After reading this book you figure you can be in the position to become mortgage free in 10 years if you buy the $300,000 house. Since the $260,000 house will require less down payment and less in monthly payments, you realize you can invest the differences of the down payment and the monthly mortgage payments. You can become mortgage free in only eight years by purchasing the $260,000 house.

If you still have a large mortgage with several years before it is paid off, you may like the idea of moving to a smaller home to reduce your mortgage principal. This may be especially true if you are retired or close to retirement.

You will be able to pay off your mortgage in much less time than with the current home you live in. This move may give you peace of mind because you know that the mortgage balance will be substantially less. However, your tax deductions will also be less. Since many people who are retired are in a lower tax bracket, the tax deductions on their home mortgage may not be as important as they were when the retirees were in a higher tax bracket.

Another benefit of moving to a smaller house is that it may be less costly to maintain. Most people, especially if retired or with financial problems, do not want to make mortgage payments. Instead, they prefer to use the money for necessities and pleasure.

Mappa Strategy Number 8
The Investment Mortgage

In Chapter 10, you read about the investment mortgage. The investment mortgage can help you pay off your mortgage early from the accumulated cash value of the specially designed life insurance policy.

Mappa Strategy Number 9
Use Other Real Estate

If you own real estate investments, such as apartment buildings, rental houses, or real estate investment trusts (REITs), you may want to invest the rental income or profits toward paying off your personal home mortgage.

Your investment property may also appreciate in value during the next several years. You always have the option to refinance or take out a loan against your investment property to pay off your home mortgage. Review all of your options with your tax advisor and financial planner.

Mappa Strategy Number 10

Make the Correct Payment on Your Adjustable-Rate Mortgage and/or Escrow Account

Do not be surprised to discover that you are making the wrong payment on your adjustable-rate mortgage. Studies have shown that between 30% and 50% of these mortgages have been incorrectly adjusted. ARMs involve changing index values and computer calculations that can allow human error. You may have been overcharged if your lender selected the wrong index date or value, rounded incorrectly, or improperly credited extra principal payments.

To assure yourself that you are not overpaying, check with your lender and ask

- for the index used;
- how the numbers are rounded;
- how many points over the index your mortgage floats;
- the day your rate changes; and,
- most importantly, the specific report from which the index is obtained. For example, if your mortgage is linked to one-year Treasury Bills, your lender could pick the rate from one of several government reports.

Many homeowners are also overpaying on their escrow accounts. This error is not uncommon and has been found on all types of mortgages.

Before refinancing or selling your home, it is important to have your mortgage and escrow account reviewed for the possibility of any errors. If you have sold your home within the last few years, you can still receive a refund if any errors were made. If you have a fixed-rate mortgage and have made prepayments, you need to make sure they have been properly credited.

To be sure that there have not been any errors made, contact your lender and request an updated statement. Once you notify your lender, regulations require that you receive the lender's response within 20 days. If you've overpaid, your lender is required to give you a refund. You can use that money for investments to help pay off your mortgage. If you want to have your mortgage professionally checked, call Loantech, Inc. at (800) 888-6781 or (301) 762-7700.

Mappa Strategy Number 11

Cancel Your Private Mortgage Insurance (PMI)

If you can cancel your PMI, you will lower your monthly mortgage payment and save money. Thus, you can invest the money that is saved.

Mappa Strategy Number 12

Consolidate All of Your Loans and Invest the Difference in Monthly Payments

Many Americans are carrying debts of $5,000, $10,000, or even more on their credit cards. A number of credit cards charge interest at rates of 14% and up to 21%. Why not take out a home equity loan to pay off all of these credit card bills or any other loans or debts? Assume you have $10,000 in credit card debt at 16% interest. You are paying $1,600 a year in non-tax-deductible interest. If you are able to obtain a home equity loan at 8% interest, your cost of funds will be 50% less than it is with your high-interest credit card debt. In fact, after taking into account the tax deduction, your cost of funds will be even less than 50%. If you are in the 33% tax bracket, the government will, in essence, pay approximately one-third of that interest cost. By obtaining an 8% home equity loan, you have now reduced your 16% interest rate charge to a much more affordable 5.36%. Imagine you have now combined all of your debts into a home equity loan and have reduced your monthly payments by $160. You can now invest that $160 every month toward paying off your mortgage.

Mappa Strategy Number 13
Continue the Same Total Monthly Payments Until All Your Loans Are Paid in Full

Let me illustrate how this strategy can help you become mortgage free much faster, and how it can also help you eliminate all of your loans and debts in a much shorter time frame. Many people have several different types of loans at the same time. For example, you have monthly credit card payments of $100 to one credit card company, $60 to another company, $200 a month payment for your car, and $150 for a home repair loan. Your total monthly payments amount to $510.

A year goes by and you have paid off the credit card that cost you $100 a month. Instead of only making payments of $410 a month ($510 less $100), you should continue to make monthly payments of $510. Instead of paying $60 monthly on the other credit card, pay $160 toward reducing the principal balance. This procedure will have this credit card debt paid off much faster than by merely paying $60 every month. Before you know it the second credit card will be completely paid off. You will then have an extra $160 available every month.

What you want to do next is to pay $160 extra every month on your car payment—instead of paying $200 you will pay $360. After your car is completely paid off you will have $360 extra every month. You still have two more years to pay off your $150 monthly house repair loan. If you apply the $360 every month, plus the required $150, your final loan will be paid off in a very short period of time.

Since you are now debt free, except for your mortgage on the house, you can invest the $510 every month. If you invest $510 a month ($6,120 per year) at 9% for 6 years you will have $50,184. The $50,184 can be used to reduce or pay off the balance of your home.

The important point here is to discipline yourself to make those $510 payments every month until you are 100% debt free. Use your personal checking account to make your monthly payments of $510. Do not use your mortgage-free checking account until you are ready to invest the $510 a month. Eventually, your goal should be to pay cash for all of your purchases, especially nondeductible interest loans. Your home or real estate investment property are the only exceptions to paying cash. Remember, the $510 you were paying every month for your debts has a lost future earnings cost for the rest of your life.

Mappa Strategy Number 14

Develop a Monthly Budget

You should develop and consistently use a monthly budget to help control spending and identify unnecessary expenditures. After developing a budget, many of my clients have increased their cash flow by several hundred dollars a month. The major benefit of using this strategy is finding unaccounted sources of money which can then be invested.

Mappa Strategy Number 15

Increase Investment Returns

Are your current savings or investments earning maximum returns? If you can increase these returns, then you will be able to accumulate money faster to pay off your home mortgage. Let us review a few areas where you may be able to increase returns on your money.

Is leaving your money in a savings account the best use of those funds? To answer this question, you must look at the after-tax and after-inflation return you will receive. Let us assume you are earning 5% in a savings account. If inflation is 4% your real rate of return is only 1%. However, the government does not look at your after-inflation rate of return but instead taxes you on the full 5%. If you are in the 33% tax bracket, you must pay 1.65% in taxes. Since your after-inflation rate of return was only 1%, when you subtract the taxes you must pay, your real rate of return is (–.65%). On a $100,000 savings account or investment earning 5%, your net after-tax and after-inflation return is a loss of $650! As you can see from this example, it can be costly to leave your money in any type of savings account or investment which has low returns.

When you are only earning 5%, what better use can you make of your money? You can invest it in municipal bonds yielding 6%. This will convert a fully-taxable 5% yield into a tax-free 6% yield (if you are investing in municipal bonds that are federal and state tax free). Over ten years, this strategy can yield a nice profit. If you like the safety of a bank, consider putting your savings or money market accounts into a certificate of deposit (CD). You will earn a higher yield on your money. However, there may be a penalty for early withdrawal on a CD. Talk to your banker. You can also invest that money in carefully selected stocks or high-quality mutual funds. Over time, your returns are likely to be much higher than if you had left the money in a savings account or other investments of this type. Remember, stocks and mutual funds have risks. Therefore, consider your risk tolerance before making any investments. The increased returns you will receive on the new investments can help you pay off your mortgage.

See your financial planner for information and advice on how to get the maximum returns on your savings and investments.

Mappa Strategy Number 16

Change Your Certificate of Deposit (CD) to a Tax-Deferred Annuity and Invest the Tax Savings

A major difference between taxable investments (such as CDs) and tax-deferred investments (such as single-premium deferred annuities) is the tax treatment. Tax-deferred annuities are becoming increasingly popular because of the tax-deferred growth advantage they have over CDs, savings accounts, money market funds, and other taxable savings instruments. Taxes must be paid on the earnings every year on a CD. These taxes are due even if you reinvest your earnings. With a tax-deferred annuity, no taxes are due until the money is withdrawn. Why pay taxes on money you do not need? It is also quite possible to earn a slightly higher rate of interest on a single-premium deferred annuity than on a CD. If you use them properly, these tax-deferred annuities can be a very effective tool for paying off your home mortgage quickly.

Imagine that you have a $100,000 CD paying 7% interest. At the end of the first year your gross return is $7,000. If your tax bracket is 33% you will net $4,690, since $2,310 went for taxes. Let us say you instead put the $100,000 into a tax-deferred annuity that was yielding 7.35%. At the end of the first year you would have earned $7,350 (no current taxes are due). As your money continues to accumulate, the difference between the CD and the tax-deferred annuity becomes even more significant. Remember, you have saved $2,310 in taxes. Why not invest these savings? Let us assume the tax savings are the same every year. $2,310 invested at 9% for 10 years will be worth $38,253. You could use the $38,253 to help pay off your mortgage.

Besides investing your current tax savings, you will also have available the value of your tax-deferred annuity. A $100,000 tax-deferred annuity at 7.35% will be worth $208,081 after ten years. A $100,000 CD at 7% will be worth only $200,966. The difference is $7,115. Also, you have to pay current taxes every year on the CD. Although your CD has accumulated to $200,966, during the ten years you spent $42,822 from your income to pay for these taxes. If you subtract the taxes paid of $42,822 from the CD's value of $200,966, you are left with a difference of $158,144. This is not the case with the tax-deferred annuity. You did not pay any taxes each year as your annuity accumulated. When you withdraw any money from your annuity you will pay income taxes at that time.

Tax-deferred annuities are not for everyone. Some have initial sales charges while others have surrender charges. Talk with your insurance agent or financial planner to find the best tax-deferred annuity for you. Let them help you find a quality annuity that has no front-end sales charge and has a relatively low surrender charge. Also, be aware of the fact that if you withdraw money from your tax-deferred annuity before age 59½, you will have to pay taxes on the withdrawal, in addition to a 10% government penalty.

Mappa Strategy Number 17

Defer Any Purchase You Do Not Need and Invest The Money

You are thinking about buying a new car. The car you would trade in is three years old. It is paid in full and basically in good condition. The monthly payments will be $415 on the new car for four years. You may want to ask yourself these questions: Do I really need it or just want it? and Will I feel more financially secure buying a new car today or owning my house free and clear in ten years or less? Why not delay buying that new car? Instead, invest the $415 every month to accumulate money toward paying off the mortgage on the house. The lost future earnings cost that would have occurred on the new car has instead turned into an opportunity gain by investing the money.

If you believe you must have a new car, why not buy a less expensive model and invest the difference. By taking this approach, you will have accomplished two goals: (1) owning a new car and (2) investing money to become mortgage free. This approach of delaying a purchase or buying a less costly item can be used for many other things you may be thinking of buying. Although it may not seem like much money at the time, I assure you that if you invest the money and let it grow (compound) year after year, it will be worth far more to you in ten years than the item you had planned to purchase. You must decide what your priorities are: an impulse item today or a paid-up house tomorrow!

Mappa Strategy Number 18
Save and Invest Money on a Regular Basis

You may be saving and investing money now on a regular basis. If you are already investing money every month, such as for college tuition, retirement, or whatever other goals you have, you should continue. If you make sound investments, your money should continue to increase. If necessary, you always have the option to use this money to help pay off your mortgage.

If you have not started a regular investment program for the exclusive purpose of paying off your mortgage, you should start as soon as possible. By investing this additional amount of money every month and combining it with some of my other strategies, you could accumulate enough money to become mortgage free in less than ten years.

Mappa Strategy Number 19
Save Money on Your Insurance and Invest Those Savings

There are a number of ways to save money on your insurance. One way is to increase the deductible on your policies. For example, you may have a very low deductible on your car insurance or your health insurance. This could be an expensive mistake. Let us say that you and your spouse each own a car with a $100 deductible. If you increase the deductible, your premiums could go down enough to make it worth investigating. Do you really want to file a claim with your insurance company for $200? If you file a few claims your rates could go up or your insurance may be canceled. Remember, you will have to pay the first $100 anyway, so you will only be receiving $100 worth of protection. Also consider raising your health insurance deductible. Assume your deductible is $250. If you increase that to $2,000 you would actually lower the premium of your health insurance enough to seriously consider making the change. In some cases, I have seen health insurance premiums go from $4,000 down to $3,000 because the deductible was raised.

More and more consumers are realizing that larger deductibles make sense and can save them money. Deposit the money you save by raising your insurance deductibles in your mortgage-free checking account and then invest it. Of course, raising deductibles is not right for everyone. Check with your insurance agent or financial planner to determine if it is right for you.

If for some reason you cannot raise your deductibles, there are still other ways you can save on your insurance costs. Many times by simply changing insurance carriers you can save from $200 to more than $1,000 per year in premiums. Let us say you selected your car insurance company eight years ago. At that time you did some comparison shopping and found out that ABC Insurance Company had some of the lowest rates. You have been with them ever since. Today, ABC Insurance Company may not have the lowest cost insurance. Maybe they had several bad claim experiences and raised their rates. Perhaps they decided they were no longer interested in business in your area. There could be many reasons that their rates are no longer competitive. It is important to continue to compare automobile premiums because companies do change them. A company that was inexpensive one year might be much higher the next. It may be worth your time to see if you can save money on your car insurance premiums. Do not forget that health insurance companies can also change their premiums. By comparing several health insurance companies, you may be able to save money on your premiums. Whatever money you save can be invested towards reaching your goal of being mortgage free.

There is still another avenue for savings in the health insurance area. Some people have highly specialized health insurance policies that may not be worth what they cost. An example is cancer insurance. You may be paying a premium for coverage you already have. If you have adequate health insurance coverage, it may pay for cancer treatment. Therefore, for many people there is no need for this additional cancer insurance. A lot of insurance is duplication of your existing coverage. When you drop unnecessary insurance, the money saved from the premiums can be invested.

It is not only the health insurance field that has unnecessary or overpriced forms of specialized insurance. The life insurance industry also has various types of specialized insurance. One type is mortgage insurance, which is usually decreasing term insurance. If you have sufficient life insurance you probably do not need mortgage insurance. The purpose of mortgage insurance is to pay off your mortgage should you die. However, if you die, your beneficiaries can use your regular life insurance proceeds to pay off the mortgage or they can do anything else they want with the money.

Another factor to consider with mortgage insurance is that the face amount often decreases as the years go by because it is decreasing term insurance. The reason for this is that as your mortgage balance decreases, less insurance coverage is needed. However, the cost of your insurance does not decrease. The premiums are the same for the term of the policy. If you feel you need this type of coverage, then shop around to see if you can save any money.

Credit life insurance is another type of coverage you may not need if you already have adequate life insurance. The purpose of credit life insurance is to pay off a particular loan or debt in the event of the insured's death. For example, you just bought a car and you are financing $15,000. If you die, the credit life insurance policy will pay off the $15,000 or remaining balance. Consider investing this money instead of paying premiums for credit life insurance.

If you own either annual renewable or level term life insurance you should compare the premiums you are now paying with other life insurance companies. There are many financially sound life insurance companies that offer inexpensive term insurance. I would recommend that you review all of your insurance coverage. You may also be able to save additional money on your life insurance and disability policies.

Savings are available on your homeowner's policy, too. When was the last time you took a really close look at your homeowner's insurance policy? You may be paying for coverage you do not need. You may be overinsured or underinsured. Review your coverage with your insurance agent or financial planner. Do not forget to make some cost comparisons with several quality insurance companies. Whatever money you save on your premiums can be invested.

It is not my goal or purpose to criticize mortgage insurance, cancer insurance, credit life insurance, or any other specialized forms of insurance. In some cases, these types of insurance might make sense. Check with your insurance agent or financial planner to discuss your personal situation. You may be surprised to learn that you will receive more protection with a smaller premium from another company.

If you combine all of these insurance savings strategies, you can invest this money where it will accumulate. You can then use it to help pay off your mortgage. Keep in mind that doing business with high-quality, low-cost insurance companies combined with having higher deductibles on your policies result in extra money in your pocket through premium savings. Make sure you put all of the money you save on insurance into your mortgage-free checking account first, before you invest it.

Mappa Strategy Number 20

Borrow from Your Life Insurance Policies

If you own cash value life insurance you can borrow money from the policy to help pay down or pay off your mortgage. Cash value life insurance is also called whole life, universal life, or variable life. Usually you can borrow up to 95% of the cash value in your policy. When you borrow money from your life insurance policy, you do not have to complete a loan application.

The net cost to borrow money from your policy is very low. Remember, you want to borrow the money and not cash surrender the policy. If you surrender the policy, you will lose your life insurance protection. I would recommend that you pay back the money you have borrowed as soon as possible. Once you have repaid the loan, you can borrow the money again to buy a car, for college tuition, or for any other reason.

The benefits of owning cash value life insurance—which you can use to become mortgage free—include:

- The cash values in your policy grow tax deferred (some insurance companies also pay dividends);
- Forced savings;
- You can borrow the money from the policy income tax free;

- If you have the waiver of premium feature and you become disabled, the cash values (dividends) will continue to accumulate, even though your premiums are waived due to your disability; and
- If death occurs, the insurance company will pay the insured's beneficiary the stated amount of insurance in the policy, which can be used to pay off the mortgage.

Cash value life insurance is the only financial vehicle that provides all of the above features in one investment. Your financial planner or insurance agent can help you decide which is the best type of cash value insurance policy for you and your family.

Mappa Strategy Number 21
Buy Term Insurance Instead of Cash Value Life Insurance and Invest the Difference from the Lower Premiums

I am a great believer in life insurance, especially in cash value life insurance. However, there are circumstances when certain people may be better off buying term insurance rather than cash value life insurance. The premiums on term insurance are less than cash value life insurance, so you would have the difference available to invest. Let us look at a situation when this may apply. If you are an experienced investor and believe you can invest your money and receive a higher return than cash value life insurance will provide, then it may make sense to buy term insurance and invest the difference from the lower premiums. If you have a profitable business, it could make sense to invest the difference in premiums back into your own business. For example, if your profit margin is 20%, you would probably want to take full advantage of this rate of return on your money. The additional money you earn can be used toward paying off your mortgage.

Most people do not invest the difference in premiums on a continual basis. Usually, the money is spent to pay bills or for other purchases. Meet with your lawyer and financial planner or insurance agent to discuss your current and future insurance needs. Your lawyer can review your estate tax situation. Your financial planner or insurance agent can cover all of the advantages and disadvantages of term insurance and cash value life insurance policies. He/she can provide you with illustrations comparing cash value insurance with term insurance and investing the difference from the lower premiums. You will then know which course of action is best for your personal situation.

Mappa Strategy Number 22
Invest the Money If You Do Not Need Life Insurance

You may not need life insurance under certain circumstances. If you have no dependents and no debts or sufficient assets to pay off the debts you do have, it may not be necessary to own life insurance. If you own a life insurance policy you are paying for the death benefit. You may want to consider investing the money instead of paying premiums. The extra money you will accumulate can be used to help pay off your mortgage.

Mappa Strategy Number 23
Start a Business in Your Home

More and more Americans are starting home-based businesses. With the easy availability of computers, modems, fax machines, and copy machines, it is now possible to run a business out of your home.

There are books available at your local bookstore or library on how to start and operate a full-time or part-time home-based business. These books will even give you ideas on many different types of businesses. You can go to conferences and seminars to learn more about your options in starting a home-based business.

If you can earn $400 a month after taxes and expenses, you can invest $4,800 a year. If you invest $4,800 a year at 9%, it will amount to $79,488 in ten years.

Mappa Strategy Number 24
Get a Part-Time Job to Earn Extra Money

I have found that paying off a mortgage can be the passion that motivates people to work longer and harder to earn extra income.

By getting a part-time job or working overtime for your present employer, the extra money you earn can be invested. For example, let us say you earn an extra $300 a month after taxes. If you invest that $300 every month at 9%, in 10 years you will have $59,616.

Remember, you do not have to work that second job or overtime forever. After you have paid off your home mortgage or accumulated enough money to pay it off, you can quit your part-time job.

Mappa Strategy Number 25
Encourage Your Spouse to Get a Full-Time or Part-Time Job

You may have thought that there was no pressing reason for your spouse to work. However, paying off your home mortgage and owning your home free and clear may be just the motivation your spouse needs.

The wife of one of my clients was very excited about this strategy. She went back to work and they are putting all of her earnings into their mortgage-free checking account and then investing the money. They will be mortgage free in only five years.

Mappa Strategy Number 26

If You Get a Raise, Invest That Money

Every year a large portion of the population receives raises. At the end of the year, many of them have very little, if anything, to show for their pay increases. In fact, some people do not even know where the money was spent. Try to avoid this situation.

If you do not need the money from your raise for bills or expenses, put the money in your mortgage-free checking account to invest. You will then have something to show for your raises. If you cannot invest the total amount of your raise, invest as much as possible.

Mappa Strategy Number 27

If You Receive a Bonus, Invest That Money

Do you ever receive a bonus from work? If you do, try to invest as much of this money as you can. Even investing a small amount every year can make a difference in helping to pay off your mortgage early.

Mappa Strategy Number 28

Invest Your Tax Refund

Many people receive tax refunds each year. What becomes of these refunds? Most people have no idea. Probably a month after most people receive a refund the money has been spent.

What if you invested your tax refund each year? After ten years, you would have accumulated money that you could use to accomplish your goal of paying down or paying off your home mortgage. Then, you would definitely have something to show for those tax refunds!

Mappa Strategy Number 29
Search for Items to Sell

I tell many of my clients that they should literally walk through their house and garage to look for items that could be sold. For example, you might come across a motorcycle that is seldom driven, a sailboat that is rarely sailed, clothing that is not worn, or tools that are no longer used. These items could be advertised in the paper or sold at a garage sale. Your profits can then be invested.

Mappa Strategy Number 30
Have Your Tax Return Professionally Reviewed

Have your tax return reviewed by a certified public accountant or a qualified tax advisor. You will have to pay a fee for their services, but the possibility of saving additional taxes may be well worth the money. The money from any tax savings is available to invest.

Mappa Strategy Number 31
Review Your Real Estate Assessment

Has your home decreased in value? If you are unsure, I recommend that you look into your real estate assessment. If you find that your house has dropped in value, you may be paying too much in property taxes.

If the value of your property has decreased and you believe your property taxes are too high, you need to challenge your real estate assessment. I recommend consulting with your tax assessor because he/she can tell you what supporting data you need to make an objection. The general rule of thumb is to show that a house of the same size in the same location with similar amenities and in the same condition as yours is selling for less than the assigned value of your property.

In addition, you should check all details of your assessment for possible errors. For example, does the assessment

- show the right number of bedrooms;
- indicate the correct square footage;
- show the right number of bathrooms; and
- indicate anything that has happened to lower the value of your property, such as road construction, a new airport, or industry development?

If you find any errors that lead to lower property taxes, you can invest those savings.

Mappa Strategy Number 32
Invest Your Inheritance

Each year, many people receive inheritances. If you are one of the these people, why not use this money for investments? After several years, these investments will have accumulated money which will help pay off your mortgage.

Mappa Strategy Number 33
Invest Any Cash Gifts You Receive

If you have a wealthy relative who may be including you in an inheritance, talk with him/her about the possibility of making these gifts while he/she is still alive. Although this can be a sensitive topic, it can be beneficial for estate tax purposes. You should consult with an estate planning attorney to discuss this situation. Any cash gifts you receive can be invested.

Mappa Strategy Number 34
Invest Your Contest or Raffle Winnings

You may get lucky by winning a contest or raffle. If you are fortunate enough to win, you should invest your winnings and watch your money accumulate.

Mappa Strategy Number 35
Invest in Tax Credit Programs

A tax credit program is a limited partnership that invests in affordable housing real estate. You will receive a dollar for dollar reduction on your taxes. These programs have suitability requirements. The general rule is that you must have $45,000 of income and $45,000 of net worth. Consult your tax advisor or financial planner to see if a tax credit program is right for you. If it is, invest your tax savings.

Mappa Strategy Number 36
Have Your Children Work for You

Pay your children a salary for helping you in your business. Since your children are in a lower tax bracket than you, the tax savings can be invested.

Mappa Strategy Number 37
Do It Yourself

Save money by doing it yourself. For example, bring your lunch to work, fix an item yourself or have a friend help you, change the oil in your car, or grow your own vegetables. Invest these savings.

Mappa Strategy Number 38
Purchase Items on Sale

If you know that you will need a certain item, shop around for the best price. You may be able to find a suitable replacement at a yard/garage sale, warehouse or discount outlet, in the paper, or by word of mouth. You can then invest the savings.

Mappa Strategy Number 39
Receive the Maximum Resale Value for Your Home

Try to maintain your home in top form so that you will be able to obtain the highest resale value. If something breaks or needs replacement, repair or replace it as soon as possible. By keeping your home in good condition, both inside and out, you should receive its full market value or very close to it. The additional money you will receive from the sale of your house can be used to help pay off your next mortgage.

Mappa Strategy Number 40
Sell Your Home Yourself

By selling your home yourself, you can save real estate broker's commissions. These savings can be invested, so that you can accumulate money toward paying off the next mortgage.

Mappa Strategy Number 41
Use Existing Savings and Investments

Many people already have savings accounts and investments. You can always apply these existing accounts toward paying off your mortgage. Assume you have a mutual fund worth $12,000 that earns 7% a year. During the next ten years it will grow to $23,520. You also have $15,000 in a certificate of deposit. If you earn 7% on your certificate of deposit, in ten years it will grow to $29,400. Between these two assets, you have available $52,920 to apply toward becoming mortgage free. Your original combined funds of $27,000 grew to $52,920 without adding any additional money.

If you decide you want to pay off your mortgage, I would strongly advise not to use all of your savings and investments. You should keep enough money liquid at all times for emergencies or other needs that may occur. Remember, after you pay off your mortgage, you should continue to save and invest money on a continuous basis for retirement or any other purpose you feel is important.

Mappa Strategy Number 42
Use Money You Have Accumulated In Your Retirement Plans

I would strongly recommend that you do not use any of your retirement money for any purpose other than for your retirement, including paying off your mortgage. However, if an emergency occurs—such as to prevent foreclosure on your home—you could consider borrowing or withdrawing money from your retirement program. If you are younger than 59½ years of age, there may be a 10% government penalty for early withdrawal from your retirement program. Also, all the money you withdraw is taxed as ordinary income. The taxes must be paid first, before you can use any of this money to pay off your mortgage.

If you are retired and withdraw or borrow money from your retirement program to pay off your mortgage, you will no longer have mortgage payments. However, the income you will receive from your retirement plan will be less because your remaining account balance has been reduced.

It is important to note that you can reduce the taxes on your retirement income by having a mortgage. You can use the tax deductions from your mortgage to help offset the income taxes that are due on the income from your retirement plan.

Some retirement plans do not allow you to borrow from their program. However, if you are able to borrow money, every effort should be made to replenish your plan's account balance as soon as possible. Always consult with your tax advisor, employee benefits department, plan administrator, or financial planner before deciding to withdraw or borrow any money from your retirement plan. Discuss in detail all of the options that are available for your own situation.

Conclusion

You need to keep in mind that your house has been amortizing. If you have a $100,000, 30-year mortgage at 9%, you would have paid off approximately 11% over the first ten years by making your monthly mortgage payments. Your mortgage balance would be paid down to $89,430. If you use only a few of these strategies, combined with the reduced principal balance from the amortization, you will be mortgage free in less than ten years.

Remember, you may owe income taxes on the earnings from your investments each year, or when you withdraw the money. You may be required to pay ordinary income tax or capital gains tax. See your tax advisor.

FINAL THOUGHTS

My goal is to teach you how to accumulate enough money so that if or when you decide to pay off your mortgage, you can do so by using the principles and strategies you have learned in this book. Before you read this book, the idea of paying off your mortgage in ten years or less without extra payments may have seemed impossible. Now that you have learned all 42 strategies, you know how this can be accomplished.

As you have learned, you can become mortgage free by making prepayments on your mortgage or by accumulating enough money to pay off your mortgage in one final lump sum payment. You have also learned that the best method of purchasing a home for most people is a 30-year mortgage. This makes the most sense for three reasons: 1) you will take full advantage of your tax deductions, 2) this length of mortgage has the lowest lost future earnings cost, and 3) you will take advantage of inflation by paying off your mortgage with cheaper and cheaper dollars each year. If you were to pay cash for a house, you would be paying for it with today's expensive dollars. You would not save any interest because you forfeit the option of investing your money in alternative investments. Plus, you have not received any tax deductions. By applying my strategies, you will have accumulated enough money to pay off your 30-year mortgage in ten years or less.

It is important to plan ahead now and apply these strategies to accumulate enough money in case you need or want to pay off your mortgage. In the event certain circumstances occur, such as retirement, you may not have the income to continue to make your mortgage payments. Even if you do have the money, you may want to use it for other purposes.

Another circumstance when you may not want a mortgage is if you have health problems. If you are sick or injured and cannot work, you could have financial problems. Making your mortgage payments could be difficult. If you have no mortgage payments, the money could be used for health care or other necessities.

There are still other circumstances when you may want to consider becoming mortgage free, such as if the home mortgage interest tax deduction is reduced or eliminated, or simply having the peace of mind that you own your home free and clear. You may want to be a homeowner, not a mortgage holder.

If you want to be in the position to become mortgage free, you should get started today. The sooner you start applying these strategies, the sooner you can accumulate enough money to pay off your mortgage whenever you choose. All of the strategies in this book are very easy to implement. Using only one strategy will help you quickly reach your goal. Applying two or three strategies will help you be in the position to be mortgage free even faster than you ever imagined. You may want to make an appointment with a qualified financial planner who can help you with the principles and strategies in this book. He/she can advise you of the best course of action for your financial situation.

I assure you that the strategies discussed in this book will work for you. They worked for me and many other homeowners all over the United States. In fact, I have received many letters from people who have used these strategies. They have expressed much satisfaction and peace of mind. I would love to hear from you regarding your accomplishments. Please write to me at American Institute for Money Management, Inc., c/o Sandy Mappa, 1701 East Lake Ave., Suite 400, Glenview, IL 60025.

I wish you success in reaching your financial goals and becoming mortgage free.

GLOSSARY

abstract of title A summary of a property's title, which includes all conveyances, grants, records, wills, and judicial proceedings and a statement of all recorded liens and encumbrances on the property and their current status. Prepared by an abstractor from a search of the title as recorded with the county recorder or other official source.

This is a written document produced by a title insurance company (in some states an attorney will do it) giving the history of who owned the property from the first owner forward. A lender will not make a loan, nor can a sale normally conclude, until the title to real estate is clear as evidenced by the abstract. In most areas of the country today, most lenders and attorneys require title insurance instead of only an abstract.

acceleration clause Provision in a trust deed or mortgage by which the lender can require that the entire balance be immediately due and payable if a specific event occurs, such as the borrower's failure to make installment payments by the due date, or sale of the property (also called an *alienation clause* or *due on sale clause*).

act of God Acts of nature that are beyond human control, such as tidal waves, earthquakes, or floods.

ad valorem Taxes based on value. The property tax is an *ad valorem* tax.

adjustable-rate mortgage (ARM) Sometimes referred to as *variable-rate* mortgage. A mortgage agreement by which the interest rate or payment is adjusted periodically (monthly or yearly) and moves up or down in conjunction with one of the widely-followed financial indexes.

The adjustment is based on an index and a margin agreed to in advance by borrower and lender. In some cases, when there are limits to the amount of change that can be made to the interest, a change may actually be made to the principal.

Such a mortgage enables a lender to match more closely its cost of acquiring funds with the return it can earn by lending them. The borrowers are enticed with a lower than normal initial interest rate and the prospect of lower monthly payments if the interest rates move downward.

adjustment date This is the day on which an adjustment is made in an adjustable-rate mortgage. It may occur monthly, every six months, once a year, or as otherwise agreed upon.

adverse possession Acquiring title to real estate by open, generally acknowledged, exclusive, and continuous possession for a statutory period of time.

affidavit of title Sworn written statement by the seller that there are no known defects in the title and he/she is in rightful possession of the property.

alienation clause This is a clause in a mortgage that usually specifies if you sell or transfer the property to another person, the mortgage becomes immediately due and payable. It is also called an *acceleration clause* or *due on sale clause.*

American Land Title Association (ALTA) This is a more complete and extensive policy of title insurance that most lenders insist on. It involves a physical inspection and often guarantees the property's boundaries. A lender will often insist on an ALTA policy with itself named as beneficiary.

American Society of Appraisers (ASA) An appraiser who displays this designation belongs to the professional organization.

amortization Paying back the mortgage in equal installments. In other words, if the mortgage is for 30 years, you would have 360 equal installments. (The last payment is often a few dollars more or less.) This is opposed to a balloon payment in which one payment is significantly larger than the rest.

amortization schedule See *prepayment schedule.*

amortize To pay back a mortgage by making periodic payments. In general, mortgages *self-amortize*, or are completely paid back by the end of their terms. An *unamortized* mortgage is one where only *interest* payments are made. At the due date, the entire *principal* borrowed must be repaid. A *partially amortized* mortgage is partly paid back over its term, but a balance (called a *balloon*) remains. That balance will have to be repaid in a lump sum, possibly requiring refinancing of the property.

annual percentage rate (APR) This represents the cost of a mortgage converted to a yearly percentage (effective interest rate) as required by truth-in-lending laws. This tells you the actual rate you will pay, including interest, loan fees, and points. Careful attention must be paid to the APR for adjustable rate mortgages. Because the APR on ARMs is calculated off of the index rate, two identical ARMs with the same rate and fees could have a different APR if the calculation was made at two different time periods, such as two weeks apart, because the index rate changed.

appraisal A professional estimate of the market value of a property. Lenders usually require that the property be valued by a qualified appraiser. It provides an estimate of the market value of the home you wish to buy based on similar homes recently sold in the neighborhood. An appraiser also will inspect the property to determine its general condition and to determine if any repairs are needed to bring the property to its full value. For example, Is the roof in good repair? The appraisal is important in determining the mortgage size a lender will be able to grant you. Lenders generally will lend you up to a certain percentage of the property value.

For example, if the appraisal is $100,000 and the lender will loan 80% of value, the maximum mortgage would be $80,000. Value is defined as the lesser of the sales price or appraisal amount. This percentage is referred to as the *loan-to-value* (LTV) ratio.

appreciation Increase in the value of a property over a period of time.

arbitration Nonjudicial settlement of a dispute by a third party.

arrears Being delinquent in paying a debt. Also, the standard method for calculating interest on a mortgage, for example, the February mortgage payment pays for January interest.

assessed value Local, city, or county governments normally place a value on a property for taxing purposes. Generally, this value only nominally reflects the current market value.

assignment of mortgage The lender may sell your mortgage without your permission. For example, you may obtain a mortgage from ABC Lender. It may then sell that mortgage to DEF Bank. You will then get a letter saying the mortgage was assigned and you may be required to make your payments to a new entity. The document used between lenders for the transfer is an "assignment of mortgage." **Note:** Beware of receiving any letter saying you should send your mortgage payment elsewhere. Unscrupulous individuals have sent out such letters to borrowers in the hopes of cheating them out of payments. Verify any such letters with your old lender. Under new laws, you should receive a disclosure at time of application and closing that indicates whether or not your mortgage will be sold. This disclosure indicates the past three years' selling pattern of the lender. The lender is also required to notify you in advance (such as 45 days) of the assignment of the mortgage and must provide pertinent information to you, such as important phone numbers of the new lender and contact names. If your mortgage is sold, the new lender cannot change the terms of your mortgage.

assumable mortgage The seller transfers his/her mortgage to the buyer who then assumes responsibility for the remaining mortgage payments. The buyer must make a down payment that will cover the difference between the selling price of the home and the balance of the assumable mortgage. The lender must approve this arrangement. Also see *assumption.*

assumption To take over an existing mortgage. For example, a seller may have an assumable mortgage on a property. When you buy the property, you may be able to take over the existing financing under its original terms and conditions. You may still have to qualify for the mortgage and pay the lender a loan assumption fee. Most conventional mortgages are not assumable. Federal Housing Administration and Veterans Administration mortgages may be assumable, but certain conditions may apply. When someone assumes your mortgage, you may still be liable if there is a foreclosure or nonpayment.

automatic guarantee Some lenders who make Veterans Administration loans are empowered to guarantee the mortgages without first checking with the Veterans Administration. These lenders can often make the mortgages quicker.

balance The amount of *principal* remaining to be paid after each mortgage payment.

balloon The *principal* amount still due when a mortgage's term ends prior to the complete repayment of the mortgage. Also see *amortize.*

balloon mortgage A mortgage that is not fully amortized and requires a large lump-sum (balloon) payment at maturity. The balloon mortgage usually provides lower interest rates due to its shorter term (usually five to seven years), and requires payment or refinancing at the end of the term. Some balloon mortgages allow for conversion of the mortgage to a fixed rate for the remaining term of the mortgage (a 5/25 balloon is fixed for five years and the borrower either has an option to pay off the mortgage in full [balloon payment], or convert the mortgage to a calculated rate for the remaining 25 years of the mortgage). Also see *two step mortgages.*

balloon payment Some mortgages are written so that the borrower is paying only the interest, and only a small or no portion of principal during the term of the mortgage. On maturity, the borrower is required to pay the entire unpaid balance of the principal in one lump sum plus any accrued interest. A fully amortized mortgage does not have a balloon payment. You should be extremely wary of such mortgages because you may not have the large balance required at the end of the term of the mortgage. Such mortgages are typically of short duration and are meant to be a stop-gap financing tool. Most home equity loans operate in this fashion.

biweekly mortgage Mortgages that are repaid at the rate of one-half of a typical mortgage's monthly payment every two weeks (26 times a year). This effectively designs in a prepayment equal to one monthly payment per year, which speeds up the mortgage's retirement and, therefore, reduces the mortgage's overall cost.

Note: Not all mortgages that are called biweeklies are, in fact, biweeklies.

blanket mortgage One mortgage that covers several properties instead of a single mortgage for each property. It is used most frequently by developers and builders.

boilerplate Standard language in deeds of trust, promissory notes, or contracts.

buydown mortgage You receive a lower-than-market interest rate either for the entire term of the mortgage or for a set period at the beginning, say two years. This is made possible by the builder or seller, or you paying an upfront fee to the lender, or building the extra cost into the mortgage. The typical buydown works like this:

Let's say the current 30-year fixed-rate is 9.5%. The type of buydown that is typically called a 2-1 buydown would start the first-year rate (which is easier to qualify for) at 7.75%. The second-year rate would be 8.75%, and the rate for the Years 3 through 30 would be 9.75%. The cost for the first two years of the buydown is recovered in the extra 0.25% charged for Years 3 through 30.

Buydowns, or purchased lower rates, are financing schemes in which a developer or seller of a real property provides a reduced interest rate charged on the mortgage by directly paying a portion of it to the lender. The lower interest rate not only attracts a larger number of prospective buyers, but also makes it easier for them to qualify for the mortgage. However, the cost of this "buydown" is usually recovered in a slightly higher price charged on the home.

buyer's closing costs Escrow costs to the buyer that include his prorated share of interest, property taxes, and other items.

call provision A clause in the mortgage allowing the lender to call in the entire unpaid balance of the mortgage providing certain events have occurred, such as your selling the property. Also referred to as an acceleration, alienation, or due on sale clause.

cap Maximum interest rate that can be charged on a mortgage. When included in adjustable-rate mortgage agreements, a cap limits how high the interest rate and/or the monthly payment can increase in a given period. There may also be a cap for the rate or payment over the length of the mortgage.

Often a cap is mandated by state or federal laws. Many adjustable-rate mortgages feature an interest rate cap beyond which the interest rate may not move. Caps can also apply to the amount your payment can change independent of the interest rate. Also see *negative amortization.*

capital gains Gain from sale of an asset of a permanent nature used in the production of income, which includes land, buildings and equipment, mineral deposits, timber reserves, patents, and many other items and excludes cash, inventory, merchandise held for sale, receivables, and certain intangibles.

capital gains tax Tax on the profit derived from the sale of a capital asset, such as a home. Gain is calculated as the difference between the sale price of the asset and the cost basis after making appropriate adjustments for closing costs, capital improvements, and allowable depreciation.

certificate of insurance Document issued by an insurance company to verify that the insured held a policy as of a given date.

certificate of reasonable value (CRV) When getting a Veterans Administration (VA) loan, the VA will secure an appraisal of the property and will issue this document establishing what they feel is its maximum value. In some cases, you may not pay more than this amount and still get the VA loan.

certificate of title Statement by a title company as to the status of the title to a property based on a review of public records.

chain of title Recorded history of ownership of the property and encumbrances affecting title. The title to property forms a chain going back to the first owners, which in the Southwest, for example, may come from original Spanish land grants.

clear title Marketable title; one free of clouds, liens, encumbrances, defects, or disputed interests.

closing When the seller conveys title to the buyer and the buyer makes full payment of the purchase price, including financing, for the property. The closing (or, in some parts of the country, settlement) is the final step where ownership of the home is transferred to the seller. Many people believe that the closing consists of sitting in a room for two hours signing papers, but the actual process includes many activities both before and after the closing meeting. Once your mortgage has been approved, a closing date will be arranged. Depending on the laws of your state, the closing may be conducted by your lending institution, a title insurance or escrow company, your real estate broker, or an attorney who represents either the buyer or the seller. Regardless of who conducts the closing, the required activities are the same.

closing costs These are expenses incurred in the course of acquiring a real property or refinancing a mortgage. In the past, these were generally an additional 3% to 6% of the mortgage amount and included loan origination fees, cost of appraisal, credit report, document preparation, filing and recording fees, title insurance premium, escrow fees, application fee, title search, deed recording, and discount points.

Closing costs may also include prorated taxes and insurance premiums. As a rule, the escrow company, the attorney, or another entity handling the closing of the transaction will render a closing statement upon the close of the escrow. Federal regulations also require that the buyer be given a good faith estimate of the closing costs by the third day after application was taken.

Recently, no points and no closing cost type mortgages have emerged. By charging a slightly higher interest rate, borrowers can literally eliminate all costs involved in the transaction. This could save borrowers virtually thousands of dollars in up-front fees in return for slightly higher monthly payments. This type of mortgage is especially attractive to borrowers who will not have the mortgage or the home for very long.

closing statement Also called a *settlement statement*. Detailed cash accounting of a real estate transaction, usually prepared by an escrow officer, broker, or attorney.

cloud on title An adverse outstanding claim, lien, or encumbrance that may affect the marketability of the title to the real property. A title insurance company will generally not give a clear title report to a property if there is a cloud on the title.

collateral (also known as security) Before a lender will make a loan commitment, it will require a sufficient collateral guaranteeing the security of its money. The house or land generally is the collateral in a real estate financing. In the event of a default by the borrower, the collateral may be seized by the lender and sold off to satisfy the loan.

commission A real estate broker's commission for the sale and purchase of a real property. This commission is usually paid out of the proceeds of the sale and reduces the amount received by the seller.

In recent years there has been a definite trend toward negotiated commissions between the seller and broker. However, most transactions carry a 6% commission on a residential property and 10% involving land. This commission is split between the seller's broker and buyer's broker.

commitment When a lender issues a written promise to you as a borrower to offer a mortgage at a set amount, interest rate, and cost. Typically, commitments have a time limit on them, for example, they are good for 30 or 60 days. Some lenders charge for making a commitment if you do not subsequently take out the mortgage (since they have tied up the money for that amount of time). When the lender's offer is in writing, it is sometimes called a *firm commitment.*

community property Law in some states that decrees assets and income acquired by a couple during their marriage are jointly owned by them.

construction loan A mortgage made for the purpose of constructing a building. The loan is short term, typically less than 12 months, and is usually paid in installments directly to the builder as the work is completed. Usually it is interest-only.

consumer protection laws When extending credit, the Equal Credit Opportunity Act (ECOA) prohibits any lender from discriminating based on race, religion, age, color, national origin, receipt of public assistance funds, sex, or marital status. In addition, ECOA requires that you be notified within 30 days of the completed application whether the application has been approved as requested, modified, or rejected. An application is considered complete once all the verifications and appraisals are given to the lender. Specific reasons for rejection must be given to you in writing.

Additional consumer protection laws include the *Real Estate Settlement Procedures Act (RESPA)* and the *Truth-In-Lending Act.* RESPA is a law that requires lenders to give you advance notice of closing costs. *Truth-In-Lending* requires lenders to disclose fully, in writing, the terms and conditions of a mortgage, including the *annual percentage rate (APR)* and other charges.

In addition, the *Home Mortgage Disclosure Act (HMDA)* requires that your lender compile and disclose specific types of information about the applicants for home mortgages that it receives. This information includes race, sex, and income, and is used to show that the lender follows fair lending practices and does not discriminate in the lending process.

conventional mortgage A mortgage made by a private institution, that is not government insured or guaranteed. Also, the term conventional mortgage applies to mortgages that meet specific criteria which enable the lender to easily sell the mortgage on the secondary market just like a stock or a bond. Agencies that purchase these mortgages, such as *Freddie Mac (FHLMC)* and *Fannie Mae (FNMA)*, basically determine the rates and guidelines for these types of mortgages. Also see *secondary market.*

convertible mortgage This is an *adjustable-rate mortgage (ARM)* that contains a clause allowing it to be converted to a fixed-rate mortgage at some time in the future. You may have to pay an additional cost to obtain this mortgage and the rate that it will convert to is usually higher than the going rate at that time.

conveyance The process of transfer of ownership or interest in a real property through a written instrument such as a deed of trust. When a note is fully paid back a full reconveyance takes place.

co-signer If you do not have good enough credit to qualify for a mortgage, the lender may be willing to make the mortgage only if you have someone (usually a close relative) with better credit also sign. This co-signer is equally responsible with you for repayment of the mortgage. (Even if you do not pay it back, the co-signer can be responsible for the *entire* balance). Today, most lenders may also require a co-signer to be on title and the mortgage making them a co-owner as well.

cost of funds index (COFI) It is just one of the index rates used to calculate the interest on adjustable-rate mortgages. The most popular COFI in the West and many other parts of the nation is the 11th District Cost of Funds, which is published once a month by the Federal Home Bank of San Francisco.

cost of not investing See *lost future earnings cost.*

counter offer A typical real estate transaction may involve a series of offers and counter offers between a buyer and seller until either there is a meeting of the minds or the negotiations are broken off. A counter offer rejects or modifies the latest offer made by the other bargaining party.

There usually is a time limit attached to an offer or a counter offer, after which it is automatically withdrawn and becomes null and void.

creative financing A term that came into increasing vogue during the days of sky-high interest rates and tight supply of money to lend. It often denotes certain unconventional and invariably flexible means of financing employed to sell a property. The seller may carry a note with a low interest rate with low monthly payments followed by a balloon payment—all done to accommodate a reluctant buyer.

credit report This is a report giving your credit history. Lenders base their expectation of how you will pay this mortgage in part on the way you have handled credit payments in the past. A report from the credit bureau shows the types of credit you have had and if you have repaid promptly. In the event that a credit report shows some problem areas, you may be asked to provide your lender with a written explanation of what caused the delinquency and what steps were taken to resolve the problem. It is advisable to contact the credit bureau to resolve the problem.

The fee for the report is usually less than $50 and you are charged for it. Most mortgage companies include both the credit report and appraisal fee in their application fee.

deed A legal document used to establish or transfer an interest in land or other real property.

deed of trust Some states use the term mortgage to denote the security interest in a real property. In a deed of trust there usually are three parties: borrower, lender, and trustee. In such a transaction, the borrower transfers the legal title to the property to the trustee to be held as collateral for the mortgage. When the mortgage is fully paid back to the lender, the note and the deed of trust are canceled. In the event of a default of the borrower, the trustee, upon instructions of the lender or beneficiary, is empowered to sell the collateral (the real property) and convey the proceeds to the lender. In most jurisdictions that use the deed of trust, the borrower is subject to having his property sold without the benefit of legal proceedings. The same states also allow the borrower to redeem the property by making the delinquent payments and reimbursing the trustee for his costs within a specified time.

default This is a technical term used to describe the breaking of the conditions of the mortgage contract. Generally, when a mortgagor has been delinquent in his monthly payments for more than 30 days the mortgagee can, at his/her option, declare the mortgage to be in default, demand accelerated payment, obtain possession of the property and start foreclosure proceedings. In most cases a default can be cured by prompt and corrective action by the mortgagor. Default may also come about by a breach of other conditions of the mortgage or deed of trust.

depreciation A real property is depreciated during a period of years using its cost basis value. The method used for computing depreciation may be a straight-line method, double declining method, or one of the other generally accepted methods. Depreciation allows a certain sum to be set aside each year to account for the gradual wear and tear of the property and eventual replacement. Land is never depreciated.

discount This term has many meanings. When you borrow from a lender, it may withhold enough money from the mortgage to cover the points and fees. For example, you may be borrowing $100,000, but your points and fees come to $3,000; hence the lender will only fund $97,000, discounting the $3,000.

In the secondary market, where the mortgage is sold much like a bond, a discount is the amount less than face value that a buyer of a mortgage pays to be induced to purchase it. The discount here is calculated based on risk, market rates, interest rate of the note, and other factors.

From a homebuyer's perspective, you can pay additional discount points to buy down an interest rate. For instance, a 30-year fixed-rate with 0 points might be 9%. However, by paying 1 discount point at closing, the lender may lower the interest rate to 8.75%.

Another form of discounting, which a consumer should definitely take advantage of, is the deeply discounted ARMs. This term generally refers to the initial term of an ARM where the interest rate being charged is lower than or discounted from where the actual current market rates are. Used properly, these mortgages can save thousands of dollars over a fixed-rate mortgage.

document preparation There are many documents that must be prepared before the closing. Some of these documents include:

1. HUD 1 Settlement Statement. An itemized list of the credits and charges, for both you and the seller, based on the contract terms.

2. Loan Documents. Final loan documents, including a promissory note, which is your legal promise to repay the mortgage; and a deed of trust/mortgage note, the instrument that is recorded in the public records, granting your lender a lien against the property to secure the repayment of your mortgage.

3. The Deed. Transfers ownership of the property to you and must contain a legal and accurate description of the property.

down payment The down payment is the upfront cash you will pay toward the purchase of your home. The down payment reduces the amount of the purchase price that will need to be financed. The standard down payment is 20%. Also see *private mortgage insurance.*

due-on-encumbrance clause This is a little-noted and seldom-enforced clause in many recent mortgages that allows the lender to foreclose if you, the borrower, get additional financing. For example, if you secure a second mortgage, the lender of the first mortgage with the clause may have grounds for foreclosing.

The reasoning here is that the lender wants you to have a certain level of equity in the property. If you reduce your equity level by taking out additional financing, the lender may be placed in a less secure position.

due-on-sale clause This is a clause in a mortgage that says the entire remaining unpaid balance becomes due and payable on sale of the property. However, many types of mortgages are assumable by the new owners if they qualify. Also see *acceleration clause*, *alienation clause*, and *call provision.*

earnest money deposit In a real property transaction, a purchaser is required to put down a certain sum of money as a good faith deposit, which is ultimately applied to the purchase price. Generally, this money would be refunded to the buyer if he/she fails to qualify for the necessary financing or if the transaction cannot be completed for no fault of his/hers. However, if he/she reneges on the transaction, depending on the exact language of the contract, he/she may forfeit to the seller the earnest money deposit as liquidated damages.

easement A right granted by a property owner to someone to use a portion of the property for a specific purpose, such as a utility easement that would allow the electric or gas company to come onto the property to check gas or electric lines.

encumbrance A legal right or claim affecting the ownership interest in a real property. An encumbrance clouds the title to the property, reduces its marketability, and diminishes its sale value. It can take numerous forms, such as mortgages, liens, unpaid taxes, pending legal action, zoning ordinances, easement rights, or restrictive covenants. A diligent title search by a title insurance company will uncover any encumbrances placed on the property. A buyer should complete the transaction only after ensuring that all encumbrances are removed and that he/she is receiving a good and clear title.

equity That portion of a property's worth that represents the fair market value less the outstanding balance of all mortgages and other *liens*. Also see *second mortgage*.

Homeowner's equity will increase as the mortgage is paid down or as the property appreciates in market value.

equity loan A loan usually placed in a second lien position, but may also be in a first lien position that is used as a vehicle for accessing extra equity in one's home. It is usually an interest-only loan that will have a balloon payment due in five to seven years. Equity loans may allow you to access more equity than a cash-out refinance because of the more liberal loan-to-value guidelines. However, careful consideration should be given to accessing an equity loan in excess of 75% to 80% of home value (first and second loan combined) due to the problem that future refinancing may be impaired. This problem is known as the "seasoning rule." Also see *second mortgage* and *seasoning rule*.

equity sharing An agreement where you have a partner or co-owner who shares the expenses and ownership of the property. Both parties may share in the appreciation of the property and the tax advantages, as well as any costs incurred.

escrow (1) Deposit by a party to a transaction of documents, money or other things of value with a third party, known as the escrow agent (such as a title company). When specified conditions are met, the escrow agent will deliver the deposited funds to another party to the transaction. The escrow agent's duties are set forth in an agreement between the agent and the parties to the transaction.

(2) Period between an agreement of terms and final settlement of conditions.

(3) Funds held in an account by a lender for purposes of paying real estate taxes or insurance.

escrow company The escrow company is the stake holder—an independent third party—that handles funds; carries out the instructions of the lender, buyer, and seller in a transaction; and deals with all the documents. In most states, companies are licensed to handle escrows. In some parts of the country, particularly the Northeast, the function of the escrow company may be handled by an attorney.

exclusion rule Federal tax-law rule that permits anyone 55 years or older a once-in-a-lifetime exclusion from tax of up to $125,000 in capital gains from sale of a principal residence.

Farmer's Home Administration (FmHA) A government-assistance program that provides mortgages to low income consumers in small towns and rural areas.

Federal Home Loan Mortgage Corporation (FHLMC) Commonly called *Freddie Mac*. It operates much like *Fannie Mae*, pooling mortgages that it buys from lenders and then selling shares in the pools to investors.

Federal Housing Administration (FHA) The FHA offers a variety of programs, the most popular of which lets you buy a house with a down payment as small as 3%.

Most area lenders are equipped to handle FHA loans. FHA loans may be preferred to conventional mortgages in that some of the underwriting guidelines are more lenient.

Federal National Mortgage Association (FNMA) Often referred to as *Fannie Mae*. This quasi-government agency purchases home mortgages from lenders, pools them with other mortgages it buys and then sells shares in pools to investors. By doing so, Fannie Mae helps to ensure that banks and savings and loan organizations have the cash they need to make new home mortgages.

final walk-through inspection Your contract should allow a final walk-through of the property 24 hours before closing. This is your opportunity to be sure that the seller has vacated the property in the manner agreed to in the contract, or, in the case of a newly constructed home, that the property is fully ready for occupancy, that all mechanical and electrical systems are working, and that any agreed-upon repairs have been made. You may be able to delay the closing if you feel these contract conditions have not been met.

first mortgage Mortgage that has priority over all other claims against the property except taxes and bonded indebtedness.

fixed interest The rate of interest remains constant for a specified period of time on the mortgage. A 30-year, fixed-rate mortgage will have an interest rate that does not change over the length of the mortgage, whereas an adjustable-rate mortgage may have an interest rate fixed for a shorter period of time such as three years on a 3-1 ARM.

flood insurance Insurance that is generally required today in addition to Homeowners Insurance when a property being financed is determined to be located in a federally mapped Flood Zone.

foreclosure The procedure used by a *mortgagee* (bank) in or out of court to force the sale of mortgaged property on which the owner has *defaulted.* The proceeds are used to repay the debt and extinguish an owner's rights, title, or interest in a property.

graduated payment mortgage (GPM) Here the payments you make vary over the life of the mortgage. They start out low, then slowly rise until, usually after a few years, they reach a plateau where they remain for the remainder of the term. This mortgage is particularly useful when you want low initial payments. It is primarily used by first-time buyers. It can be and often is used in combination with a fixed-rate or adjustable-rate mortgage.

grant deed Type of deed used to convey real property. Contains warranties against prior encumbrances or conveyances.

growing equity mortgage This is a rarely used type of mortgage where the payments increase according to a set schedule. The purpose is to pay additional money into the principal and, thus, pay off the mortgage earlier and save interest charges.

hazard insurance Property insurance that covers hazards such as floods, fires, or windstorms. Also see *flood insurance*.

home equity line of credit See *second mortgage*.

home equity loan See *second mortgage*.

home improvement loan A loan to finance the repair, modernization, or improvement of residential real estate.

impound account Money held by a lender for payment of taxes, insurance, or other debts against real property. The funds in the impound account are generally accumulated through deposits made to it each time you make a mortgage payment. Also see *escrow account*.

index A mutually agreed-upon, regularly published interest rate totally out of the lender's control, against which lenders compare and then adjust the interest rate and monthly payment on adjustable-rate mortgages. There is a wide variety of indexes used, including Treasury bill rates, cost of funds to lenders, and others.

inflation An abnormal increase in available currency and credit beyond the proportion of available goods, causing a sharp and continuing rise in price levels.

insured loan Loans insured by either a government agency or a private mortgage insurance company.

interest A fee paid to a lender for the privilege of borrowing money, usually expressed as an annual percentage rate (such as 10%).

investment mortgage An interest-only loan that combines a specially-designed universal life insurance policy with a mortgage.

joint tenancy Interest in real estate owned by two or more persons with rights of survivorship. Title is held as if all the owners collectively are one person. On the death of one of the joint tenants, the surviving tenants receive the deceased tenant's interest by the right of survivorship. Consequently, the decedent's interest cannot be transferred by will or descent.

junior lien A lien recorded subsequent to another lien. A junior lien holds a lower priority than a senior and would be paid only after all senior liens have been satisfied.

land contract Conveyance by which the buyer takes possession of the land but the seller retains title until the buyer completes installment payments for the purchase of the property.

lease with option to buy The buyer will make regular rental payments to the seller. A portion of each monthly payment will be applied toward the down payment. When enough money has been paid to cover the down payment, the property can then be purchased.

leasehold interest The right to use a property under certain conditions, but it does not include the right of ownership.

lien This is a legal claim placed against a property to ensure payment of a debt. As part of the process of obtaining a mortgage, the borrower gives the lender a lien on the property being financed. Should the homeowner *default*, the lien holder can *foreclose*. A creditor may place a judgment lien, a taxing authority may place a tax lien, and unpaid contractors and mechanics may place a mechanic's lien until their debts are paid by the homeowner. A lien creates a cloud on the title and would normally require them to be cleared before the property can be sold.

loan assumption Process by which a buyer purchases real estate by assuming an existing mortgage and agreeing to personally repay the debt. Some assumable loans may or may not release the original mortgagor from liability. Also see *assumable mortgage* and *assumption*.

loan commitment Written agreement by a lender to lend a certain amount of money at a specified rate of interest for a certain period of time.

loan origination fee This is a fee charged by a lender at the time of making the loan and is usually represented as points or a percentage of the amount borrowed. Technically this is interest prepaid and the Internal Revenue Service allows the loan origination fee to be a deductible expense that may or may not be amortized over the length of the mortgage. Also, points paid are usually deducted only when they were paid in conjunction with the purchase of a principal residence.

loan-to-value ratio (LTV) The percentage of the appraised value or purchase price of a property that a lender will loan. For example, if your property is appraised at $100,000 and the lender was willing to loan $80,000, then the loan-to-value ratio would be 80%.

lost future earnings* cost The loss of earnings on money that could have been invested. The lost opportunity by not investing.

lost investment of future earnings (LIFE of your money) See *lost future earnings cost*.

* *Lost future earnings* and *loss of future earnings* are interchangeable. In this book, we will use lost future earnings.

lost opportunity cost See *lost future earnings cost.*

MAI—American Institute of Real Estate Appraisers An appraiser who has this designation has passed rigorous training.

margin An amount, calculated in a percentage, that a lender adds to an index to determine how much interest you will pay during a period for an adjustable-rate mortgage. For example, the index may be at 7%, and the margin, agreed upon at the time you obtained the mortgage, may be 3%. The interest rate for that period, therefore, would be 10%.

mechanic's lien Lien given as security for payment of labor and materials.

MIP A few lenders use this acronym when they are talking about a *mortgage insurance policy.* However, most bankers use the term when they are talking about the fees you must pay for private mortgage insurance—in other words, your *mortgage insurance premium.*

The Federal Housing Administration and conventional lenders require a mortgagor to buy mortgage insurance under certain circumstances. For instance, when a borrower is able to pay less than the normal down payment while purchasing a property, the lender may require additional security in the form of private mortgage insurance. This is an additional cost to the borrower and continues until such time as the lender agrees to release the borrower from having to pay it or until the mortgage is refinanced with enough equity having accumulated to avoid having to pay it again. The bank may be willing to release the MIP if the borrower agrees to pay for a new appraisal and the new appraisal reveals enough equity in the property to release the MIP. However, the lender is not required to release the MIP.

mortgage A pledge of property as security for repayment of a loan. This term is commonly used to refer to the loan itself. Defined as a claim or lien against the real property given by the buyer to the lender as security for payment of a loan.

mortgagee The bank or lender who lends the money to the borrower for the purchase of a real property. The mortgagee holds the note until the debt is paid back.

mortgagor One who pledges property as security for a debt: the borrower.

negative amortization or deferred-interest loan When the payment on an adjustable-rate mortgage is not sufficiently large to cover the interest charged. When this happens the borrower is given the choice of sending in the additional interest payment, or having the excess interest added to principal; thus, the amount borrowed actually increases. The amount the principal can increase is usually limited to 125% of the original mortgage value. Anytime you have a cap on the mortgage payment, you are looking at a mortgage that has the potential to be negatively amortized.

origination fee Today, this usually refers to one of the costs to you when you obtain a mortgage. In the past, it has meant a charge that lenders make for preparing and submitting a mortgage. It originally was used only for Federal Housing Administration and Veterans Administration loans where the mortgage package had to be submitted to the government for approval. With a Federal Housing Administration loan, the maximum origination fee used to be 1%. Today, it is possible to obtain a 0-point mortgage and even a 0-cost mortgage from most lenders.

personal property Any property that does not go with the land. This includes automobiles, clothing, and most furniture. Some items are disputable, such as appliances and floor and wall coverings. Also see *real property*.

PI Principal and interest portion of a monthly mortgage payment.

PITI (Principal, Interest, Taxes, and Insurance) These are the major components that go into determining your monthly payment on a mortgage. (They leave out other items such as homeowner's insurance, association dues, utilities, and so forth). If a lender requires an impound account, taxes and insurance would be collected on a monthly basis and would be paid directly when they are due.

As a general rule, a lender will not give you a mortgage if your PITI exceeds 30% (also known as LTV ratio) of your gross monthly income. However, there are many portfolio lender products available that will exceed these guidelines.

pledged account mortgage A large deposit is paid by the borrower or any other interested party to the lender at the time of the loan origination. This deposit is invested in an account that will earn interest. The deposit will subsidize the mortgage interest payments over the beginning years of the mortgage, which will result in lower payments in the early years. The lender will withdraw an amount every month that is equal to the difference between what the borrower must pay and the actual value of the mortgage at the full interest level. Payments rise gradually over a number of years until they reach their full level which is the market rate. Then the mortgage becomes a standard ARM or FRM. The rate and monthly payments will change based upon the contract.

points A point is equal to 1% of a mortgage amount. For example, if your mortgage is $100,000 and you were required to pay 2½ points to get it, the charge to you would be $2,500. Some points which you pay when obtaining a mortgage may be tax-deductible.

Lenders use the term *basis points*. A basis point is 1/100 of a point. For example, if you are charged ½ of a point (.5% of the mortgage), the lender will think of it as 50 basis points.

Competitive conditions, money supply, and the borrower's credit worthiness will determine the number of points demanded by the lender. For instance, a non-owner occupied property purchase would command a slightly higher interest rate and higher than normal points from the lender. The borrower usually has to pay the lender the points at the closing.

portfolio lenders These are lenders and programs that do not necessarily meet the Federal National Mortgage Association (FNMA) or Federal Home Loan Mortgage Corporation (FHLMC) mortgage guidelines. Many times self-employed borrowers or borrowers with low down payments, high debt ratios, or blemished credit may need a portfolio lender product to qualify for a home mortgage.

pre-closing activities The purpose of closing is to make sure the property is properly ready and able to be transferred from the seller to the buyer. To ensure that the transfer can be made, prior to closing it is necessary to receive:

1. Title Search and Report. Research of land records, court records, and other legal documents to determine if the seller has a clear, marketable title to convey to the buyer.

2. Title Insurance. Indicates the results of the title search and assures the lender that the title to the property qualifies for a policy of title insurance.

3. Survey. Confirms that the property's boundaries are as described in the purchase and sales agreement. This may not be required in certain instances.

4. Termite, Well, Sewer, or Septic Certificates. Certifies that the sewage system and water supply work properly and that the property is free of termites and/or other wood-destroying insects. The sales contract will determine whether the buyer or the seller is responsible for the above inspections and certificates.

5. Mortgage Title Insurance. You will need to provide title insurance for your lender by your closing. It is also advisable for you to purchase a separate title insurance policy that covers your interest. Title insurance protects you and your lender against losses that may be incurred because of a defect in the title, a forgery, a recording error, claims of undisclosed or unknown spouses or heirs, and other risks that did not appear in the public records when the title search was done.

6. Hazard Insurance (sometimes referred to as a homeowner's policy). You are also responsible for obtaining homeowner's insurance prior to closing and for providing proof of insurance to your lender. This insurance will protect you and the lender from loss in the event the home is damaged or destroyed by fire, storm, or other hazards. If your property is located in a Flood Zone, the lender may also require a separate flood insurance policy.

prepayment A payment in advance of its due date, frequently used to mean payment of principal in full. The term "prepayment" also implies small advance payments applied toward the outstanding balance of the mortgage at regular or irregular intervals.

prepayment penalty This is a charge made by the lender to the borrower for paying off a mortgage early. In times past (more than 25 years ago) nearly all mortgages carried prepayment penalties. However, those mortgages were also assumable by others. Today virtually no fixed-rate mortgages (other than Federal Housing Administration or Veteran's Administration) mortgages are truly assumable and hence, almost none carry a prepayment penalty clause. Even the lenders who do impose a prepayment penalty generally allow a certain amount to be prepaid every year without incurring any penalty.

prepayment schedule A chart showing each mortgage payment broken down into its interest and principal components. The balance due after crediting the principal portion of the payment is also normally shown. Also called *amortization schedule.*

price-level adjusted mortgage Variation of a fixed-rate mortgage in which your mortgage payment stays the same in real dollars (adjusted for inflation). The concept is that you are repaying the money you borrowed from the lender at its real value. There is a major difference between this and a traditional fixed-rate mortgage: The borrower assumes all of the risk for the price level changes, and therefore the lender is willing to lend its money at a lower rate.

principal The sum of money that was borrowed or remains due. The outstanding debt against which interest is being charged is referred to as the principal. On prepayment schedules, the word principal means the component of that month's payment that is applied toward the equity of the mortgage.

private mortgage insurance (PMI) By paying an initial fee, plus a monthly premium, homeowners who cannot afford the normal 20% down payment can put down as little as 3%. Once your equity increases past the 20% point, you may be able to stop your PMI payments. (Also known as *MIP*).

It is important to remember that PMI does not protect you—instead it protects your lender. If you eventually default on your mortgage, the insurance policy will kick in and reimburse the bank for some or all of its losses if it is forced to foreclose.

It is written by an independent third-party insurance company and typically covers only the first 20% of the lender's potential loss. PMI is normally required on any mortgage that exceeds 80% LTV ratio.

purchase money mortgage When you get a mortgage to cover part of the purchase price of a home. This is as opposed to getting a mortgage through refinancing. In some states, no deficiency judgment can be obtained against a borrower of a purchase money mortgage. If there is a foreclosure and the property brings less than the amount borrowed, you as a borrower cannot be held liable for the shortfall.

purchase offer An offer made to purchase real estate by a potential buyer. This is a legally binding contract and would contain terms and conditions of the offer and any other contingencies. It is usually accompanied with a good faith deposit which, if the offer is accepted, would be applied toward the purchase price.

quit-claim deed Deed of conveyance in which the grantor transfers all of his/her interests in the property without making any guarantees. Used to release property from claims to facilitate the transfer of title.

Real Estate Settlement Procedures Act (RESPA) This act requires lenders to provide you with specified information as to the cost of securing financing. Basically, it means that before you proceed far along the path of getting your mortgage, the lender has to provide you with an estimate of costs. Then, before you actually sign the documents binding you to the mortgage, the lender has to provide you with a breakdown of the actual costs.

real property Real estate. This includes the land and anything appurtenant to it, including the house. Confusion often exists when differentiating between real and personal property with regard to such items as floor and wall coverings. To determine whether an item is real property (goes with the land), certain tests have been devised. For example, if curtains or drapes have been attached in such a way that they cannot be removed without damaging the home, they may be spoken of as real property. On the other hand, if they can easily be removed without damaging the home, they may be personal property. It is a good idea to specify in any contract whether items are real or personal. This avoids confusion later on.

reconveyance The transferring back of title of property from a second (usually temporary) property owner to the previous owner. Once a debt has been repaid, a reconveyance takes place, and the title reverts to the previous owner (the person who incurred the debt).

recording fee A fee charged by the county or city recorder's office for recording a document. Deeds, liens, default notices, or abstracts of judgments are recorded in a local office where land records are maintained.

refinancing Refinancing occurs when a mortgagor pays off an existing mortgage with the proceeds of another mortgage. If the current mortgage was obtained at a higher interest rate than presently available, a homeowner may wish to refinance the property at a lower interest rate and lower his/her monthly payments and total interest costs. Refinancing may have its own costs too, such as loan origination fee and other closing costs.

regular prepayment A set amount sent in every month along with the monthly mortgage payment, for example, $25 a month.

renegotiated mortgage A variation of the balloon mortgage. The interest rate is fixed for a pre-determined time after which the interest rate is negotiated. Also see *balloon mortgage.*

reverse mortgage A reverse mortgage is a home loan in which the money goes from the lender to the homeowner, instead of the homeowner having to pay the lender each month. He/she will receive all or part of the equity out of the home in cash while continuing to live in the house. The homeowner has the option to receive a certain amount of money each month or establish a line of credit.

seasoning rule Term used to describe the age of a mortgage (a mortgage that is five years old is "well seasoned"). A seasoned mortgage has established payment history and credit. The seasoning rule also applies to the amount of time that has elapsed since a borrower pulled out cash from the equity of the property. An example of a seasoning problem would be a borrower who takes out an equity mortgage and draws on it within a year of refinancing the home. He/she may have a loan-to-value problem which could cause the refinance to be denied.

second mortgage Available for some portion of the difference between the property's market value and the balance due on the first mortgage. Recently, home equity lines of credit have taken the place of second mortgages. With a home equity line of credit, you generally have the right to borrow up to a specified limit. But remember: Second mortgages/home equity loans place a lien on your home. If not paid back in accordance with your agreement, your property may be foreclosed.

Such a mortgage is additional financing obtained by the property owner usually at a higher interest rate for a shorter period of time. Second mortgages would occupy a junior position to the first mortgage in the event of a default. Many lenders will not offer second mortgages, insisting instead on firsts only.

secondary market Various governmental agencies such as the Federal Home Loan Bank or Federal National Mortgage Association routinely buy mortgages written by private lenders and repackage them for sale on the open market that is known as the secondary market. This brings added liquidity to the mortgage market by making more money available for lending.

security Same as collateral. Lenders require a borrower to put up a security (usually the home) to ensure that a mortgage will be repaid. In the event of a default, the security is seized and sold to pay off the mortgage.

shared appreciation mortgage The buyer must agree to share with the lender an established amount of the home's appreciation after a pre-determined number of years, or at the time of sale or transference.

Society of Real Estate Appraisers (SREA) This is a professional association to which qualified appraisers can belong. Whenever you hire an appraiser, you are encouraged to look for a minimum of the SREA designation.

subject to This is a phrase often used to indicate that a buyer is not assuming the mortgage liability of a seller. For example, if the seller has an assumable mortgage and you, the buyer, "assume" the mortgage, you are taking over liability for the payment. On the other hand, if you purchase "subject to" the mortgage, you do not assume liability for payment.

subordination clause A clause that can be inserted into a mortgage document that keeps that mortgage secondary to any other mortgages. Mortgages are valued according to the chronological order in which they are put onto a property. The first mortgage on a property is called a "first" in time. The next mortgage put on is a "second" in time. The next a "third" in time, and so forth. The order is important because in the event of foreclosure, all the money from a foreclosure sale goes to pay off the lender of the first. Only if there is any left over does it then go to pay off the holder of the second. Only if there is any left over after this does it goes to pay off the lender of the third, and so forth. The earlier the number of the mortgage, the more desirable and superior the mortgage is considered.

Normally, when a first mortgage is paid off, the second advances to become the first, the third to the second, and so on. However, since some lenders only offer first mortgages, having a second advance to the first position could prevent you from refinancing with a new first—unless the second and other inferior mortgages were fully paid off. You might not want to do this. Therefore, a subordination clause can be inserted into the second and other inferior mortgages. It specifies that the mortgage will forever remain in its current position, thus allowing you to pay off the existing first and get a new first.

This technique used by developers who give the sellers of land a second mortgage and then get a new first for construction. Today, most institutional lenders either will not allow a subordination clause inserted in any second or inferior mortgage they make; or if they do subordinate, they will limit the amount of the first.

title This is evidence that you actually have the right of ownership of real property. It is in the form of a deed—there are many different types of deeds—that specifies the kind of title you have, for example, joint or common.

title company Company that provides title insurance for real property.

title insurance policy This is an insurance policy that covers the title to your home. It may list you or the lender as a beneficiary. It is issued by a title insurance company or through an attorney underwritten by an insurance company and specifies that if for any covered reason your title is defective, the company will correct the title or pay you up to a specified amount, usually the amount of the purchase price or the mortgage.

Before issuing such a policy, for which either the buyer or the seller or both (as determined by local custom) must pay a fee, the title insurance company investigates the chain of title and notifies all parties of any defects, such as liens. These must then be paid off. Sometimes, if it is not desirable to pay them off (as in the case of old bonds), a policy of title insurance with an exception may be issued.

Most states have standard title insurance policies. For example, California has a *CLTA*, or policy approved by the *California Land Title Association*. It may not be a very complete policy and may not give you total coverage. A more complete policy is the *ALTA*.

title search A tracing of the title to a real property through public records to verify that the owner does own the property and has a right to sell it.

two-step mortgage This allows payment at a fixed interest rate for five or seven years, then adjusts to a new interest rate that remains fixed for the remaining 25 to 23 years. Also see *balloon mortgages*.

underwriting The process of reviewing all the information gathered and making a judgment of the level of risk involved in granting the mortgage. It is a picture in time that analyzes the value of the property, your ability to pay, and your willingness to repay the mortgage. It is in the best interest of both the lender and the borrower to avoid mortgages that are difficult to repay.

During the underwriting process, the lender reviews the:

- debt-to-income ratios (28%/36%);
- credit history;
- loan-to-value ratio;
- stability and likelihood of continued employment;
- appraisal of property; and
- cash reserves.

uniform settlement statement Statement required in a transaction covered by the *Real Estate Settlement Procedures Act (RESPA)*. Requires disclosure to borrowers, lenders and sellers of settlement costs and disbursement of closing and selling costs.

Veterans Administration (VA) This federal agency also provides a variety of services and runs the VA loan program—the one that allows veterans to purchase a house with no down payment.

Most lenders will loan up to $184,000 under the VA program. You can get more information by talking with local lenders, mortgage brokers, or mortgage bankers. You can also find the nearest branch of the Veterans Administration in the "United States Government" listings in the white pages.

Veterans Administration (VA) loan A mortgage guaranteed by the Veterans Administration. The VA actually only guarantees a small percentage of the amount loaned, but since it guarantees the first amount loaned, lenders are willing to accept it. In a VA loan, the government advances no money; rather, the mortgage is made by a private lender such as a bank.

warranty deed Deed in which the grantor warrants clean title to the property.

wrap-around financing Here a lender blends two mortgages. If the lender is a seller, then he/she does not receive all cash. However, instead of simply giving the buyer-borrower a simple second mortgage, the lender combines the balance due on an existing mortgage (usually an existing first) with an additional mortgage. Thus, the wrap includes both the second and the first mortgages. The borrower makes payments to the lender who then keeps part of the payment and in turn makes payments on the existing mortgage.

The wrap is used typically by a seller who either does not trust the buyer to make payments on a first or who wants to get a higher interest rate. This relieves the buyer from having to look for new financing which may be hard to come by or may be too costly.

ABOUT THE AUTHOR

Sanford L. (Sandy) Mappa is President of the American Institute for Money Management, Inc. (Glenview, Illinois), the President of Mappa Financial Planning, Inc. (Glenview, Illinois), a Registered Investment Advisor, a stock broker, and insurance broker. He has more than 20 years of experience counseling individuals in the investment and financial planning field. He has received several of his profession's top awards. Sandy has earned the following eight designations and certifications:

- Certified Financial Planner (CFP)
- Registered Financial Consultant (RFC)
- Accredited Estate Planner (AEP)
- Chartered Financial Consultant (ChFC)
- Chartered Life Underwriter (CLU)
- Registered Health Underwriter (RHU)
- Certified Fund Specialist (CFS)
- Certified Investment Specialist (CIS)

Sandy has appeared on television and radio. His career has included hosting "Mapping Your Financial Future," a weekly financial planning and investment radio program, writing a financial planning newspaper column for the Lerner newspapers (Chicago), and appearing in the *Chicago Tribune*, *Chicago Sun Times*, *Money* magazine, and *Consumer's Digest*. In addition, Sandy has taught adult education courses on financial planning at Roosevelt University (Chicago), Governors State University (University Park, Illinois), and the United Credit Union (Chicago).

Sandy is an instructor for the National Center for Financial Education (San Diego). He is also a member of the

National Speakers Bureau. In addition, Sandy holds memberships in several financial planning associations.

Sandy has conducted financial and business planning seminars for many professional groups, corporations, and businesses. Most recently, Sandy has conducted nationwide educational seminars to teach his proven mortgage-free strategies to financial planners, insurance agents, stock brokers and mortgage brokers.

establish a line of credit at bank that has your home mortgage. If you are disabled, or lose job noone will give you loan except by using equity in house

per mo

15 yr $336 — difference = 252
30 yr 590 — + 33% tax = $83

$335 total savings per mo as diff between 30 yr & 15 yr mortgage

if invest the $335 per mo at 10%, at end of 10 yrs, have $64,279
12 yrs $86,248
15 yrs $128,146

use this as backup

i.e. invest 30 yr mortgage save difference between 30 & 15 yr mortgage

if you have long time to save money - put money in equities - will get more money than bonds or cash or CD's